# The Creativity Toolkit

# The Creativity Toolkit

*Provoking Creativity in Individuals and Organizations*

**H. James Harrington**

**Glen D. Hoffherr**

**Robert P. Reid, Jr.**

**McGraw-Hill**

New York   San Francisco   Washington, D.C.   Auckland   Bogotá
Caracas   Lisbon   London   Madrid   Mexico City   Milan
Montreal   New Delhi   San Juan   Singapore
Sydney   Tokyo   Toronto

# McGraw-Hill

*A Division of The* **McGraw·Hill** *Companies*

1 2 3 4 5 6 7 8 9 0 DOC/DOC 9 0 1 0 9 8 7

ISBN: 0-07-913730-X


**Library of Congress Cataloging-in-Publication Data**

Harrington, H. J. (H. James)
    The creativity toolkit : provoking creativity in individuals and
organizations / H. James Harrington, Glen D. Hoffherr, Robert P.
Reid., Jr.
      p.    cm.
    Includes bibliographical references.
    ISBN 0-07-913730-X
    1. Creative ability in business.   2. Organizational change.
3. Thought and thinking.   I. Hoffherr, Glen.   II. Reid, Robert
(Robert P.), Jr.   III. Title.
HD53.H374   1997
658.3'14—DC21                    97-36698
                                       CIP


The sponsoring editor for this book was Philip Ruppel. The editing supervisor was John M. Morris, and the production supervisor was Suzanne W. B. Rapcavage. Production was managed by John Woods, CWL Publishing Enterprises, Madison, WI. It was designed and composed at Impressions Book and Journal Services, Inc., Madison, WI.

McGraw-Hill books are available at special quantity discounts to use as premiums and sales promotions, or for use in corporate training programs. For more information, please write to the Director of Special Sales, McGraw-Hill, 11 West 19th Street, New York, NY 10011. Or contact your local bookstore.

# Contents

# About the Series

*The Creativity Toolkit* is one title in McGraw-Hill's Harrington's Performance Improvement Series. The series is designed to facilitate an organization's Performance Improvement Management (PIM) process. It provides insight into the most useful approaches now available to bring about improvements in organizational performance as measured by:

► Return on investment,
► Value added per employee, and
► Customer satisfaction.

Each title in the series is written in an easy-to-read, user-friendly style to reach employees at all levels of an organization. Our goal is to present complex methodologies in a way that is simple but not simplistic. The following are other subjects covered in the books in this series:

► Statistical Process Control
► Process Redesign
► Process Reengineering
► Establishing a Balanced Scorecard
► Reliability Analysis
► Fostering Teamwork
► Simulation Modeling
► Rewards and Recognition
► Managing the Change Process

We believe that the books in this series will provide an effective way to learn about these practices as well as a training tool for use in any type of organization. In each title in the series, the design features a series of icons in the margins that call your attention to different points. Use these icons to guide your reading and study:

Requirement, Rule, or Principle

 Discussion

 Concept or Idea

 Example

 Guide

 Quote

 Definition

 Exercise

It is our hope that you will find this series of Performance Improvement Management books enjoyable and useful.

H. James Harrington
Principal, Ernst & Young LLP
International Quality Advisor

# About the Authors

**Dr. H. James Harrington** is one of the world's quality system gurus with more than 45 years of experience. He has been involved in developing quality management systems in Europe, South America, North America, and Asia. He currently serves as a Principal with Ernst & Young, LLP and is their International Quality Advisor. He is also chairman of Emergence Technology Ltd., a high tech software and hardware manufacturer and developer.

Before joining Ernst & Young LLP, he was president of the consulting firm Harrington, Hurd, and Riecker. He was a Senior Engineer and Project Manager for IBM, and for almost 40 years, he worked in quality function. He was chairman and president of the prestigious International Academy for Quality and the American Society for Quality Control. He has released a series of videos and CD ROM programs that covered ISO 9000 and QS-9000. He has also authored a computer program on benchmarking, plus members' video tapes on performance improvement. He has written ten books on performance improvement and hundreds of technical reports.

The Harrington/Ishikawa Medal was named after him in recognition of his support to developing nations in implementing quality systems. China named him their Honorary Quality Advisor, and he was elected into the Singapore Productivity Hall of Fame. He has been elected honorary member of seven quality professional societies, and has received numerous awards and medals for his work in the quality field, including the 1996 Lancaster Award from ASQC in recognition of his work to further the Quality Movement internationally.

**Glen D. Hoffherr** is a senior consultant for James Martin Government Consulting. He has spent over 20 years in management in the high technology industry. For the last eight years he has been a consultant and author focusing on strategic planning, organizational design, change management, and creative decision making.

He has authored, co-authored, or been a contributing author to more than 15 books and numerous magazine articles. He is an animated, interesting, and entertaining speaker who has lectured at national and international conferences on five continents, and at numerous colleges and universities around the world.

He has worked with organizations in many fields including local, state, and national government, foreign governments, telecommunications, high technology, service, manufacturing, health care, and software.

**Robert P. Reid, Jr.,** is a dynamic and innovative presenter, with over 30 years experience as an educator, author, speaker and organizational developer. Reid has written extensively in the areas of organizational change management, creative thinking, and systems design. He has worked with more than one hundred major organizations on six continents, and has conducted courses and seminars at seventeen universities. His ability to communicate complex systems issues in a clear non-threatening fashion is recognized world-wide.

# Dedication

I dedicate this book to my wife, Mary, whose patience, caring, and understanding made it possible for me to be creative; and to my parents, Ed and Laura, who made it all possible.

I would also like to thank all of those who provided their comments and ongoing support during our work on this book.

Bob, Jim and I set out to develop a graphic-rich, creative book on creativity, that would provide a resource for those who think in different contexts.

Working with Bob and Jim has been a mind expanding experience for all of us.

*Glen Hoffherr*

# Acknowledgment

I want to acknowledge the many contributions made by Mary E. Hoffherr for her work in helping pull this book together; and to Loria Kutch for helping proofread, prepare the CD-ROM storyboard, and coordinate the inputs.

I would also like to recognize Ari Kugler, COO of SystemCorp's operations, for funding the CD-ROM development; and Richard Rosenbloom, also from SystemCorp, for preparing the CD-ROM.

We would be remiss in not acknowledging Charles Mignosa who developed and recorded the relaxation part of the CD-ROM.

*Jim Harrington*

# Foreword

## Creativity in Action

When children are very young, they seem naturally creative. They have spontaneity and an ability to see and interpret the world in new and original ways. But as they grow up, learning social conventions and accepted ways of seeing and interpreting the situations in which they find themselves, they seem to lose this natural creativity. What's really going on, however, is not a loss of creative ability but rather a decline in the need to use that ability to get along in the everyday world. At least from a conventional perspective, it seems that way. This is unfortunate because conventional approaches to dealing with experiences usually result in conventional, often mediocre outcomes. We all still have the ability to generate novel, original, and creative solutions that can help us solve problems permanently, make our processes operate much better, and dramatically increase customer satisfaction, and sometimes open up whole new markets.

*Organizations—and especially individuals in them—need to start re-imagining themselves. Personal and corporate futures can change if people will once again start tapping into their creative skills, which have sat dormant for so long.*
MICHAEL JONES

So how do you access your natural creativity? In a world filled with conventional thinking, it isn't easy. Fortunately, many tools are available to help you transcend the usual way of understanding problems—and opportunities—and come up with creative responses that can make a big difference in your success. In this book we call those tools *mind expanders*. We think of them as suspenders for our minds, that help us keep our creativity in place.

 **Dd**
This is a sample of the text for the definition, or these are more synonyms and usages that are commonly found in the English language.

**Mind expanders** These are exercises, approaches, or tools that help an individual or team think differently about situations and generate creative ways to deal with them.

Although it's important to be able to come up with creative ideas, such efforts are for nought unless the ideas are implemented in ways that result in desired outputs. We call those implementation efforts *innovation*. Creativity without innovation is wasted effort, yet innovation cannot occur unless the creative process has been fulfilled first. In other words, creativity and innovation are intimately connected. Because the English language does not have a word that denotes the integration of creativity and innovation, we will use the word *creativity* to cover both of these processes.

 **Dd**
This is a sample of the text for the definition, or these are more synonyms and usages that are commonly found in the English language.

**Innovation** This is the act of converting a creative concept or idea into an output.

Today, we sometimes seem to be faced with an infinite amount of information. A single issue of the Sunday *New York Times* contains more information than a person a century ago might have acquired over a lifetime. No matter what situation we encounter, there seem to be data or techniques available to deal with it. Breakthroughs, truly creative approaches, are few and far between. Creative efforts today are more evolutionary than revolutionary. We tend to refine concepts and techniques.

In a way, we are almost victims of our information wealth. With this vast knowledge base, people today either already have ready answers to problems or will do research from current knowledge to find them. This is not bad. In fact, it is smart to gather information about others' approaches to similar problems and how their solutions might help you or members of your organization. However, this knowledge can also hold us back from taking advantage of our creative powers to invent whole new ways of dealing with problems and situations. If less information were readily available, we would be obligated to rely more on our creativity. There is an inverse relationship between creativity and the amount of information and knowledge we have: the more information, the less necessity to be creative. However, there is a fallacy at work in this relationship. There is always room for creativity; there is always the possibility of breakthrough. However, making a breakthrough requires suspending conventional thinking and engaging your creative power. How do you do that? That's what this book is all about.

# Engaging Your Creative Power

On a fishing trip to Canada, we were traveling across a cow pasture in a new Buick and hit a rock. The rock ripped out the plug in the car's oil pan. Luckily, we were only about a half mile from our Indian guide's sod home. We managed to push the car and finally get it to his yard. Our trip seemed to be ruined. It was more than 60 miles to the nearest gas station that could replace the oil pan. We tried to figure a way to get the pan off with pliers and a monkey wrench—all the tools we had—so we could try to repair it, but we had no luck in doing that. Our guide told us to stop worrying about the car and go fishing. He volunteered to have his wife, who had about a dozen kids running around, fix it. With no alternative, we took off fishing.

When we returned seven days later, our guide's wife had repaired the oil pan without anyone's help. This temporary repair was still holding two weeks later when I had the oil pan replaced. Before we reveal the solution (it appears in Appendix B), see if you can figure out how she did it.

In conclusion, I invite you to consider these observations about creativity by an unknown author:

The abilities that are characteristic of creativity can be developed. They include:

► The ability to wonder, to be curious.
► The ability to be enthusiastic, spontaneous, and flexible.
► The ability to be open to new experience, to see the familiar from an unfamiliar point of view.
► The ability to make desirable but unsought discoveries by accident. This is called serendipity.
► The ability to make one more thing out of another by shifting functions.
► The ability to generalize in order to see universal application of ideas.
► The ability to find disorder, to synthesize, to integrate.
► The ability to be intensely conscious yet in touch with subconscious sources.
► The ability to visualize or imagine new possibilities.
► The ability to be analytical and critical.
► The ability to know oneself, and to have the courage to be oneself in the face of opposition.
► The ability to be persistent, to work hard for long periods in pursuit of a goal without guaranteed results.
► The ability to put two or more known things together in a unique way, thus creating a new thing, an unknown thing.

Want to know more? Read on.

CHAPTER | **1**

# Overview:
# Becoming More Creative

*"Unless you're number one, you have to innovate."*
LEE IACOCCA, PRESIDENT CHRYSLER CORP.

## The Creativity Problem

People are born with an abundance of creativity and get a great deal of satisfaction out of using it. Given this fact, why is the lack of creativity such a problem around the world? Well, there are three reasons:

▶ Education that minimizes the need to be creative
▶ Lack of exercising our creative powers
▶ Avoidance of risk

## Education that Minimizes the Need to Be Creative

Today's world is so rich in data that we cannot afford the luxury of letting everyone create his or her own database. If everyone were allowed to gener-

1

ate individual basic concepts without some degree of standardization, we would not be able to interact with one another effectively. For example, imagine how hard it would be to communicate if each person spoke a unique language—or how hard it would be to pay bills if every individual used a different numbering system.

Often, the very education that helps us function in this complex world keeps us from conceiving truly creative solutions. Education does not make an individual creative. In fact, it has just the opposite effect on the individual because there is less need to call on creative powers on a continuous basis because someone else has already provided the answers. Of course, being educated does not preclude being creative. However, highly creative, educated individuals do not rely on education to solve their problems; they use it to develop new, improved solutions.

Because of the complexity of today's environment, we start limiting children's natural creative urges very early in life by saying, "Don't try to be creative. We already have an answer that is better than anything you can create." Jim Harrington, one of the authors of this book, relates the following story.

My son Jim, at age three, wrote "NTP." When I asked him what it was, he replied, "That's 'Mom and Dad, I love you.'" My reply was, "That's good, Jim. We love you, too. Let me show you how to write 'Dad.'" In my love for my son, I wanted him to learn to conform to accepted practices and stop being creative. But from a higher level, he had created a breakthrough that reduced a twenty-letter sentence to three letters. Yes, education and training mean a form of repressed creativity: "Don't create a language; I'll give you one. Don't create an alphabet; copy this one. Don't create new; memorize the old one."

That's what education (in contrast with learning) is all about: maximizing and memorizing what is already known, not creating the new. We are not suggesting that education is bad. In fact, we feel just the opposite. The more knowledge an individual has, the better he or she can perform. The problem is that while we are collecting knowledge, we are not creating. The figure shows what we mean.

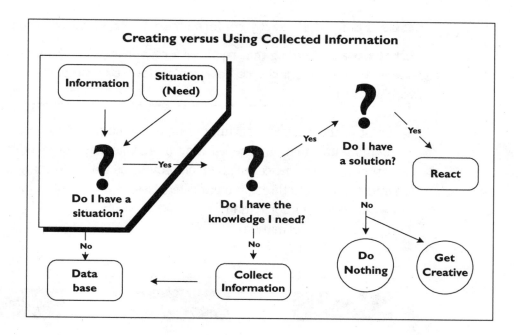

Creating versus Using Collected Information

**Knowledge** consists of intellectual mental components acquired and retained through study and experience.

**Information** is constrained and narrower in scope than knowledge; it implies a random collection of material rather than orderly synthesis.

**Wisdom** is an understanding of what is true, right, or lasting. It involves sound judgement and the ability to apply what has been acquired mentally to the conduct of one's affairs.

*"It is a characteristic of wisdom not to do desperate things."*
    HENRY DAVID THOREAU, NINETEENTH CENTURY AMERICAN WRITER

**Fact** is something that is known with certainty. It has been objectively verified.

**True** is defined as exactly conforming to a rule, standard, or pattern.

**Situation** is anything that requires a response. It can be a problem that needs to be solved, a choice between options, or a simple need to make a verbal response.

Most of the time, the learning process is going on, and we are accumulating more information. The learning process is made up of education, observation, and experience, all of which provide us with information. We filter the information into three different categories.

► Knowledge information
► Wisdom information
► Unneeded information

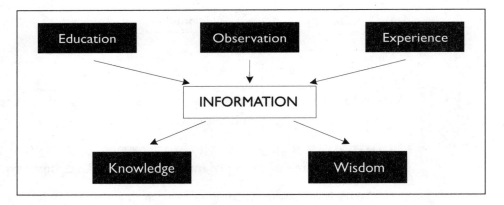

The wisdom and knowledge information is stored into our database. It is important to understand that the wisdom database is a subset of the knowledge database. The knowledge database includes both true and false information, but the wisdom database contains only true information. The unneeded information is rejected and not stored in the left-hand side's database.

When the brain recognizes that a situation requires a reaction, it asks, "Do I need more information to handle the situation?" If the answer is yes, it instructs you to do more research before you react to the situation. You remain in this cycle until you have collected the required amount of information or until you give up on collecting more information.

When you have sufficient knowledge, you react to the situation. Whether you rely on your available knowledge or need to collect new information, you may find yourself stuck using it in the same old way because your assumptions are conventional and have never been challenged. You may need an outside catalyst to help you break out of your conventional perspectives.

*Inspiration is the impact of a fact on a prepared mind.*
LOUIS PASTEUR

In medieval times, the court jester was such a catalyst. In a number of organizations today, individuals serve this function. The court jester's job is to ask questions and present possibilities in a way that opens people's minds to possibilities they had not considered.

*The Lord gave us two ends—one to sit on and the other to think with. Success depends on which one we use the most.*
ANN LANDERS

If you don't have enough information, it is usually because of one or more of the following:

► The information takes too long to get.
► The information is not available.
► You believe a better solution exists.
► You get more satisfaction from creating a new solution.

The major problem we have with our database is that more than 90 percent of the information is out of date (five years old or older), and only a very small proportion of it is based on facts. We are often misled by teachers and other so-called experts who present concepts that are based on statistically unsound and unproved databases. As a result, the solutions that are generated are often not the optimum solutions.

Once we decide that we have enough information in our database, we use our accumulated knowledge and wisdom to answer the question, "Do I have an acceptable solution?" If the answer is yes, we proceed with implementing the solution. If the answer is no, we have only two options:

Option 1: Ignore the situation and do nothing.
Option 2: Develop a new, creative approach to react to the situation.

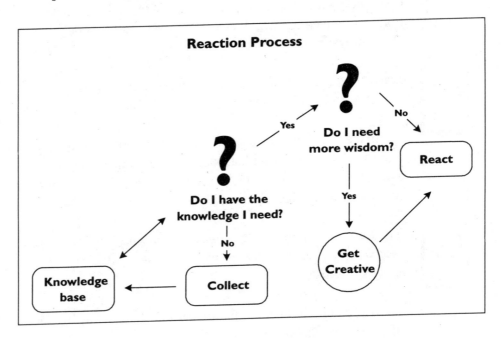

In the last case, you use all of your available knowledge and create a new solution. It is easy to see that as you analyze more information, there is less need to be creative because you have the required knowledge to react to the situations you are encountering.

# Lack of Exercising Our Creative Powers

Individual creative capabilities are a lot like physical capabilities. The more you use them, the better you can perform. If you don't exercise those capabilities, they diminish very fast. Just as you have a physical exercise program to shape up muscles not used in your normal activities, you need a creativity exercise program that stimulates the brain tissues that are used too seldom today.

# Avoidance of Risk

Creative people are willing to take risks to challenge rules, expected behaviors, and the status quo.

**The status quo** is a condition in which the environment and the individual's expectations about the environment are in harmony. It does not mean that the individual's expectations are being met.

There is an old Japanese saying: "The nail that sticks up the highest is the first to be driven down." We'd like to reword this statement to say, "The nail that sticks up the highest is the first to get noticed." The individual or group that is creative stands head and shoulders above the others that surround them. Of course, when you think of challenging the status quo, you realize the dangers of failing and of being different from the rest. A conservative individual trying to compete against a creative individual is at a great disadvantage. It is a lot like a five-foot-tall individual competing for a spot on a professional basketball team. As Woody Allen put it, "If you're not failing every now and again, it's a sign that you are not doing anything very innovative." Too many people spend their lives worrying about failing and, because of that, live in a mire of mediocrity. They are afraid to change. Confucius once said, "Our greatest glory is not in never failing, but in rising every time we fall."

**Change** is a condition in which an individual's expectations are no longer aligned with the environment. Change occurs when expectations are not met.

To be truly creative, you must be willing to take risks, to risk it all on an idea or a belief. We are not talking about sky diving or Indy car racing or rock climbing. We are talking about the risks we need to consider when we depart from doing the same things in the same ways. Thinking differently (and in some cases, acting differently) does involve an element of risk—risk in the sense that one might be embarrassed, ridiculed, left out, talked about, or whatever else may happen when one stands out from the norm. As shown in the figure below the more radical the creative idea, the higher the risk.

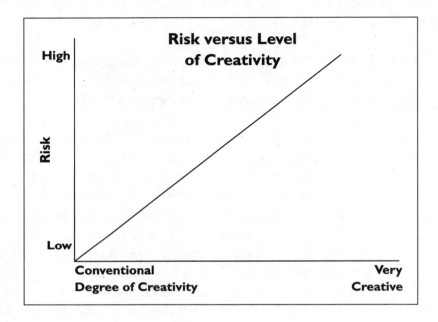

The following are comments made about some creative and/or radical ideas.

*I confess that in 1901, I said to my brother Orville that man would not fly for fifty years. . . . Ever since, I have distrusted myself and avoided all predictions.*
WILBUR WRIGHT, U.S. AVIATION PIONEER, 1908

*I must confess that my imagination . . . refuses to see any sort of submarine doing anything but suffocating its crew and floundering at sea.*
H.G. WELLS, BRITISH NOVELIST, 1901

*Airplanes are interesting toys but of no military value.*
MARSHAL FERDINAND FOCH, FRENCH MILITARY STRATEGIST AND FUTURE WORLD WAR I COMMANDER, 1911

*The horse is here to stay, but the automobile is only a novelty—a fad.*
> A PRESIDENT OF THE MICHIGAN SAVINGS BANK ADVISING HORACE RACKHAM (HENRY FORD'S LAWYER) NOT TO INVEST IN THE FORD MOTOR CO., 1903. RACKHAM IGNORED THE ADVICE, BOUGHT $5,000 WORTH OF STOCK, AND SOLD IT SEVERAL YEARS LATER FOR $12.5 MILLION.

*Everything that can be invented has been invented.*
> CHARLES H. DUELL, U.S. COMMISSIONER OF PATENTS, 1899

*Who the hell wants to hear actors talk?*
> HARRY M. WARNER, WARNER BROTHERS, 1927

*There is no reason for any individual to have a computer in their home.*
> KENNETH OLSEN, PRESIDENT AND FOUNDER OF DIGITAL EQUIPMENT CORP., 1977

*Nobody now fears that a Japanese fleet could deal an unexpected blow on our Pacific possessions. . . . Radio makes surprise impossible.*
> JOSEPHUS DANIELS, FORMER U.S. SECRETARY OF THE NAVY, OCT. 16, 1922

*What use could this company make of an electrical toy?*
> WESTERN UNION PRESIDENT WILLIAM ORTON, REJECTING ALEXANDER GRAHAM BELL'S OFFER TO SELL HIS STRUGGLING TELEPHONE COMPANY TO WESTERN UNION FOR $100,000

*Computers in the future may . . . perhaps only weigh 1.5 tons.*
> POPULAR MECHANICS, FORECASTING THE DEVELOPMENT OF COMPUTER TECHNOLOGY, 1949

*We don't like their sound. Groups of guitars are on the way out.*
> DECCA RECORDS REJECTING THE BEATLES, 1962

*Radio has no future.*
> LORD KELVIN, SCOTTISH MATHEMATICIAN AND PHYSICIST, FORMER PRESIDENT OF THE ROYAL SOCIETY, 1897

*[Television] won't be able to hold on to any market it captures after the first six months. People will soon get tired of staring at a plywood box every night.*
> DARRYL F. ZANUCK, HEAD OF 20TH CENTURY–FOX, 1946

*For the majority of people the use of tobacco has a beneficial effect.*
Dr. Ian G. Macdonald, Los Angeles surgeon, quoted in Newsweek, Nov. 18, 1963

*Heavier than air flying machines are impossible.*
Lord Kelvin, president, Royal Society, 1895

*Ruth made a big mistake when he gave up pitching.*
Tris Speaker, 1921

Our society is strongly biased toward conformity and conservatism, with everyone expected to stay within certain boundaries. Those who cross these boundaries are considered different and are in some way punished. But thinking differently requires moving and thinking beyond these boundaries. We need to find ways to do this without endangering our mental selves. Being willing and able to take these risks is an essential step toward becoming creative.

Consider what you do—what almost everyone does—when riding in an elevator. You walk into the elevator, turn around, push the button for the floor you want, then stare either at the floor or at the changing floor numbers. Because of the "rules of elevator riding," you don't say anything. You notice that few people talk, even if they know each other. Next time, take a risk and say something. Perhaps say, "I'm sure glad we're all going the same way" or "We are all certainly quiet today." If it's crowded, ask someone to push the floor button for you. You don't need to be a stand-up comic. But you need to try out your risk muscles by doing something different that will help you think about the world in new ways. If you really want to take a risk, don't turn to face the front of the elevator. Stand looking at the other passengers and wait for them to say something.

## Lost Opportunities

Let's examine another situation. You are in a meeting (a class or a staff meeting, for example), and someone makes a statement that you don't understand. What do most people do? They keep quiet, hoping that someone else will ask for clarification or that the cryptic statement will be explained later;

usually, however, this never happens. Take a risk and ask the question. In almost every case, others will have the same question you do. (This risk is especially difficult if the speaker is someone of higher rank.) Think of Tom Hanks in the movie *Big.* He took risks that most of us would not because the barriers that we normally avoid had been eliminated through the switch that had taken place. The age/creativity relationship had been changed.

In situations like the one just described, there is always an element of potential intimidation, even if unintentional. You see taking the risk as possibly subjecting yourself to ridicule (all eyes turning to you as if to say, "How come you don't understand?" or any number of things that you can imagine). Fear of that risk keeps you sitting silently. You follow the rule drummed into you in childhood: "Don't speak unless spoken to." The elevator, the meeting, and other similar situations give us opportunities to use our risk muscles to think differently and to act differently. Thinking and acting go hand in hand because acting will strengthen our thinking.

## How Do You Know You Are Creative?

A question we are frequently asked is "What is the difference between creative thoughts and normal thoughts?" A simple answer is that you are not being creative when you are doing something the same way it was done before and getting the same results. Typically, you will know you are creative by the way you feel about the results of the activity.

One experience that results from being creative is sometimes called "the Wow experience" because it is accompanied by an expression or feeling of "Wow, that's great" or "Wow, look at what I've done." The "Wow experience" is a true high. It will build spirit, enthusiasm, confidence, and contentment.

The "Wow experience" is more satisfying than the strongest drug or narcotic that is being smuggled into the U.S. today. It's a lot like the feeling you get from having sex, only it lasts a lot longer.

Other typical emotions are embodied in the expressions

▶ "Aha!"

▶ "Hey, that's great!" and

▶ "Eureka!"

# Key Issues Calling for Creativity

In our daily lives, we all address three different types of issues: setting a direction, planning how to move in that direction, and accomplishing the tasks that will lead in that direction.

When you deal with direction issues, you are trying to answer questions like "Where am I going?" and "Why am I going there?"

The second issue, planning, is so essential day to day that we often do it without even thinking about it. Most of the time we do a poor job of planning because we don't think enough about it. If we want to succeed, we must learn to set aside adequate planning time. At the personal level, when you are engaged in planning, you are trying to answer questions like "How will I get where I am going?" and "What are all of the steps I must take to reach my goal?"

Setting directions and making plans are preliminary to completing tasks. Most of us find that completing tasks takes up at least 80 percent of our time. With regard to task issues, you are trying to answer questions like "What must I do to follow my plan?" and "What can I do differently to make my life easier?" In our experience, we have found that each of us spends about 3 percent of her/his time setting directions, 17 percent of his/her time making plans, and 80 percent of his/her time completing tasks, which include reacting to problems that should not have occurred if we had done a good job of planning. Creativity can and should be applied in all three of these areas. However, the greatest rewards of creativity are usually found when we focus it on the tasks that we accomplish.

# Is It Good or Is It Bad?

You can improve your creativity by learning about and using tools that help you see and understand the world from new perspectives.

So you've just had what you think is a really creative idea. What do you do with it? Do you just share it right now so everyone will know you are creative, or do you wait and check it out? The answer is yes. Both choices are right, depending on the idea and the environment in which you find yourself. If the idea is very important and will have impact on other people, you may want to sit on it for a day or so and maybe even check it out with some friends to see if they can spot a weakness that you had not detected.

In some circumstances, you will get only one chance to sell a concept, so you must present it right the first time. At other times, spontaneous sharing is the best approach. You should develop a systematic way to evaluate your ideas before deciding how to react. The following are typical questions that are helpful in evaluating an idea:

- ► Do you really understand the situation? So often, a creative idea fails because it does not address the situation at hand.
- ► Will your idea address the situation in a way that solves a problem or makes an improvement?
- ► Is your idea the best action that can be taken?
- ► What are the advantages of your idea over the present situation?
- ► What are the advantages of the present situation over your idea?
- ► What will it take to implement your idea?
- ► Who will need to approve your idea before it can be implemented?
- ► Who will need to implement your idea?
- ► Is your idea in line with the current culture?
- ► Is this the right time to discuss your idea?
- ► How long would it take to implement your idea?

# Rising above the Immediate

Too often we define a path of action, then spend all our time justifying that path rather than breaking down perceived barriers that we have built around ourselves. Imagine being in a canoe, paddling down a winding river in eagerness to reach the sea. You can be so intent on paddling that you follow a long loop in the river, failing to realize that you could have shortened your journey by a mile if you had portaged 20 feet. The truly creative person will take a global view of the river to define the optimum path—in contrast to the hard-working conventionalists who reason, "The harder we paddle, the faster we'll get there." Moreover, the creative person will welcome the input of outsiders who can help him or her perceive the problem in different terms.

The creative person is willing to take both a global view (often called synthesis) and an analytic view. The ability to look at the same idea from more than one viewpoint is very difficult to master, but it is well worth the effort. In later chapters, we will provide a number of tools and techniques to help you learn how to approach any situation from many viewpoints.

# Myths about Creativity

As children, we heard stories of ghosts and goblins, witches and vampires, dragons and heroes; soon, we lost sight of fact and reality. In school, we were taught that if something is printed in a book, it is fact. We tend to accept without question anything told us by a person who has "Dr." in front of his or her name. We draw conclusions from statistically unsound databases. We have a friend from India who is a superb mathematician, and we conclude that all Indians are very systematic thinkers. My wife sees a movie about a chainsaw murderer, and for months she worries every night when I am away. We have a penchant for developing beliefs that often have no basis in facts, but we hold them so strongly that our ability to see the reality becomes severely limited. The following are some myths related to creativity, along with comments on the validity of these beliefs.

**Creativity is a God-given gift.** This is a half-truth. Nature gives us our mental capabilities. The way we use our thought patterns is based on the environments we live in, our individual interests, and our personal drive.

**Only some people are creative.** Everyone has the ability to be very creative unless he or she has a severe mental handicap. We all can be creative if we are just willing to work at it. It is usually easier to follow than to lead, but it is never as satisfying.

**If there's a lot of it, it must be creative.** We often connect bulk with creativity, when in truth, creativity usually results in reduced bulk. A person who can present a concept in one sentence is far more creative than one who requires pages to present the same concept.

**There's no need for me to be creative.** If we do the same old thing in the same old way, the best we are going to get is the same old, poor results. Everyone has to develop his or her creative powers not only to survive in a very competitive working environment but also to meet the challenges that face us in family life. We don't all have to write books or paint pictures, but we all hang pictures, buy presents, plan vacations, and basically sell our-selves to the rest of the world. The rules, education, and experiences we have accumulated over the years may be our meat and potatoes, but the creative ways we use those experiences become our dessert.

**Creativity is always good.** Creativity can be both bad and good. Hitler was a very creative individual, as was Michelangelo. One man's cre-ativity led to the Holocaust whereas the other man's creativity led to world-wide enlightenment. If one uses creative powers to manipulate and take ad-vantage of others, this is clearly not good in most people's eyes. Conversely, most would agree that creativity that helps people perform better or develop something new and useful is clearly good.

**Creative people are successful people.** This is not necessarily so. Often, very creative people do not have the ability to sell the fruits of their creativity and/or do not care whether anyone makes use of their ideas. Cre-ation without implementation is a futile exercise and can be more discourag-ing than encouraging.

## Truths about Creativity

It is important that we all understand what creativity is and what it is not. The following basic concepts will help define creativity.

**Creativity is not a single process.** Creativity is a number of differ-ent processes that make up a system. A creative idea may come to you in a blinding flash or through a very deliberate approach that refines your thought patterns.

**Your creativity powers can be improved.** Methods are available today that will allow you to exercise your creative powers and change the way you think, enabling you to become a much more creative person.

**Creativity is often an explosion rather than a logical sequence of information.** Some of the very best ideas may occur on the golf course or in the shower: All of a sudden, you get a flash of inspiration. Be prepared for those flashes. Don't tuck your idea in one corner of your mind, saying, "I'll get back to it later." Write the idea down immediately.

**Creativity is random.** Although you can't predict when you'll have a creative breakthrough, you can increase the frequency of such breakthroughs by having a prepared mind and by understanding the processes for enhancing the likelihood of producing creative ideas.

**Frustration is often the father of creativity.** Most people take the easy way out and search for rules that will allow them to complete specific assignments or solve specific problems. When our rules fail and we have no place to go, creativity kicks in.

**Creativity is seeing the same old thing in a different light and/or in new combinations.** Many of the techniques you will read about in this book, in fact, are designed to help you change the context in which you view a problem or opportunity or to recombine elements in a way that leads to creative breakthrough.

**Creativity is risky but rewarding.** Doing a job in the way your predecessor did it or the way your boss told you to do it gives you a way out: If problems arise, you can always blame them on somebody else. This approach requires no thought and results in little progress. Only when we use our creativity to improve do we truly make progress and become recognized as superior performers by our associates. In addition, we enjoy a feeling of self-satisfaction that is never present when we are blindly following someone else's lead.

**Creativity is the ultimate source of self-indulgence and self-satisfaction.** When you exercise your creative powers, you develop a sense of self-confidence and self-worth. This is a way of proving to yourself that you are adding value to the rest of the world.

**The way you performed in the past does not always reflect your potential.** The fact that you have not been creative in the past does not mean that you cannot be creative in the future. Likewise, some people who have been creative look backward and stop being creative as they mature. The will to create must be renewed every day. "You cannot earn today's paycheck on the basis of last week's press clippings."

**Trust your own observations.** Don't be limited by others. Too often, someone in a higher position or someone we respect influences our thinking in a way that prevents us from applying our personal creative powers. Encouraging diversity rather than conformity is the key to creativity. It brings out many ways of understanding the same phenomenon and the possibility of building on one another's ideas.

**Creativity often kicks in when you reject your first acceptable solution.** People tend first to look at a problem and define how it can be solved, then to collect information related to that solution that proves it is the right one. For any important problem, you should develop at least three alternate solutions before the best-value solution is defined.

**The more you use your creative powers, the better they work.** The brain is a muscle; like any other muscle, it must get exercise to stay in shape.

**Creativity turns work into fun.** Too often, we wear our conformity masks and are afraid to relax. We envy children who have fun at everything they do. We complain about our daily chores. We complain that it's too hot in the office when the temperature rises above 80 degrees. But we stop on the way home to play tennis in the 90-degree sun and enjoy the experience. Let's free up our creative powers. Let's turn the monotony of daily chores into a series of enjoyable experiences.

# Common Creativity Killers

Are you a creativity killer? Do you encourage creative thoughts or repress them? A newly hatched idea is fragile. We need to encourage it, cultivate it, and help it develop and grow, not casually discard it. The following are 13 commonly used phrases that discourage creative thinking. We hope you don't use any of them.

- ► It won't work.
- ► It makes me afraid.
- ► We tried that already.
- ► That can't be done.
- ► It will never work here.
- ► Let's be serious.
- ► That's ridiculous.
- ► What's original about that?
- ► How dumb can you be?

► You obviously don't understand the situation.
► That's a silly idea.
► That's impossible.
► Who died and left you boss?

*We can't build a better tomorrow by using yesterday's methods. Businesses that expect to make it in today's global marketplace must begin by tapping the creativity of all employees, not just a few maverick inventors or dynamic CEOs. Competitive advantage today comes from continuous, incremental innovation.*

HAROLD R. MCALINDON

# Rules for Becoming a More Creative Individual

Here are 13 techniques that individuals can use to utilize creative abilities more effectively.

► Create pictures in your mind, and turn these pictures into reality.
► Keep your mind open to new ideas by presenting new experiences to your senses. Be a keen observer of your environment. Provide the mind with the raw materials that it needs to be creative.
► Do something creative each day. Set aside a specific time each day to review the creative things that you've accomplished.
► Define alternative approaches to situations and problems. Don't use a one-track approach and gather data to prove you were right. Focus your creativity on simplifying the old and new approaches.
► Maintain a questioning attitude. Remember, there is always a better way. If you don't find it, someone else will—and will use it as a steppingstone to get ahead of you.
► Don't be afraid to take risks. You will never fulfill your true potential if you play it safe.
► Record your ideas as soon as you get them. Keep a note pad with you at all times.
► Take time to relax and unwind. Take a long walk or a leisurely hot bath. Play golf or listen to restful music. Try meditation or yoga.

► Don't accept limiting factors as being unchangeable without challenging them with all your vigor.

► Gain confidence and enthusiasm by first focusing your creative efforts and ideas on things that are within your control to implement.

► Help others be creative by pointing out the strengths, not the weaknesses, of their ideas. We already have too many devil's advocates. Be an angel's advocate.

► Find your creative time of day. Some people are morning people; others are evening people. We all function differently. Sample your emotions and creative powers to determine when you are most creative. Then, set that sacred time aside to work on developing new concepts.

► Start today to improve your creative processes. It has been said, "Yesterday is history, tomorrow is a mystery. Today is a gift. That's why it's called the present."

*I am a great believer in luck, and I find the harder I work, the more of it I have.*
STEPHEN LEACOCK

# Your Creative Powers

As we begin to explore many techniques that you can use to turn on your creative powers, remember these affirmations about you and others like you that serve as a foundation for our ideas:

► We are confident that you are or can be creative.

► We are confident that you can improve your creativity. It has been estimated that Leonardo DaVinci and Thomas Edison used less than 50 percent of their potential creative capabilities.

► We are confident that regular use of the mind expanders described in this book will improve your creativity.

► We are confident that risks, creativity, and rewards go hand in hand.

► We are confident that in the twenty-first century, creativity will become more critical to real success than ever before.

► We are confident that creative people get more joy from life.

▶ We are confident that if you do not use your creative powers, you will become less capable of using them.
▶ We are confident that real success goes to creative people who can implement their ideas and concepts.

Everyone can be creative; however, most people feel that they are not creative. It is up to you to make yourself more creative. We will provide you with a number of tools and techniques, but only you can make them work.

# Innovative Organizations

We have pointed out that creativity is an individual trait. Put creative people together in small groups (departments), and you get originality. Put small groups together into organizations, and you get innovative organizations. That's what Bill Gates did at Microsoft, becoming the richest man in the world at age 40. In a *Fortune* magazine survey of senior U.S. executives, 39 percent of the respondents indicated that Microsoft was the most innovative organization in the United States. A very distant second was General Electric with only 18 percent of the votes. The top ten–rated innovative organizations in the United States, in order, are

1. Microsoft
2. General Electric
3. 3M
4. AT&T
5. Motorola
6. Apple Computers
7. Intel
8. Merck
9. Wal-Mart Stores
10. Chrysler

What sets these highly innovative organizations apart from the rest of the population? By looking closely at the way these organizations are managed, we see seven key elements that contributed to their innovative environments:
▶ Respect for individuals, their rights and dignity
▶ Aggressive performance-related measurements for everyone

- ▶ Encouragement of constructive dissatisfaction
- ▶ Low level of fear existing throughout the organization
- ▶ Failure viewed as a learning process
- ▶ Technology used as an enabler rather than as a driver
- ▶ Innovators who are encouraged, recognized, and rewarded

## Constructive Dissatisfaction

Of the six characteristics mentioned, one—constructive dissatisfaction—requires explanation. Most organizations would feel that they were performing poorly if they had dissatisfied employees. We don't agree with that view. Sure, we do not want employees who are complaining and moaning. That is destructive dissatisfaction. The innovative organization has people who are not satisfied with doing their jobs the same old way. They are always challenging the system, looking for a better way of delivering the same desired output. These constructively dissatisfied employees do not accept answers to their suggestions like

- ▶ That's the way it's done here.
- ▶ We tried that years ago, and it didn't work.
- ▶ We'll think about that at a later date.
- ▶ The boss wants it done that way.

*Speak now or forever hold your peace."* —Everyman

*Dr. M. George Allen, retired vice president of research and development at 3M Corporation, put it this way: "You obtain innovation by doing three things:*
- ▶ *Encouraging innovators,*
- ▶ *Recognizing innovators, and*
- ▶ *Rewarding innovators.*
*The process of encouraging innovators is never-ending. Push people to stretch beyond their limits . . . even at the risk of failure. Treat mistakes not as failures but as learning experiences."*

Constructively dissatisfied employees are the ones who are saying, "Things can be different. There is a better way to do it, and I'm going to find it." Destructively dissatisfied employees state, "Things are bad; everything's fouled up. This place doesn't operate well."

The difference is that the constructively dissatisfied employees have the personal belief that they can make things better, that there is a better way, and they are committed to finding it. These employees are the ones who are not only challenging the status quo but also identifying how it can be changed. IBM used to call these people "wild ducks." Management, on a whole, does not like to manage wild ducks because they challenge management's set pattern. It is much easier to have people snap to attention and say, "Yes sir. I'll do it your way." As a result, management spends more time clipping the wings of the wild ducks than encouraging them to fly. This is an unfortunate situation because it is these wild ducks who are going to make your organization great. Sure, the wild ducks fail more often than the domesticated ducks. But they are the ones who make the big breakthroughs. Take the time to identify these wild ducks and encourage them to jump out of the comfortable nest that too many of us sit in.

# Innovative Organizations Look Different

Innovative organizations encourage their people to be creative. Such an organization is quick to recognize a new, creative idea and nurture the creative seed, watering and fertilizing it until it is a blooming, fruit-laden tree. You find these organizations all around the world. In France, there's Renault; in Japan, Sony; in the United States, 3M. In Italy, it is Fiat. These organizations not only have creative people but they effectively transform the creative ideas into revolutionary new products. Many organizations are effective at generating new concepts but ineffective at transforming them into valuable products. Texas Instruments is a good example of an organization that has been very creative but relatively ineffective at transforming its concepts into competitive advantages. Creativity is defined as the generation of new ideas.

Innovation is doing new things. There is a big difference between thinking up a new story line and transforming the story line into a book. Many people are quick to realize this difference when someone else comes up with a successful new product and they realize this was the same idea they had in the past but never brought to fruition. Creativity without innovation equals lost opportunities and discouragement.

Organizations that combine creativity and innovation create real value and significant competitive advantage. Organizations that are truly creative look at the concept development process and the related risks in a very unique way as shown in the figure. Creative organizations evolve every concept through these five distinct steps.

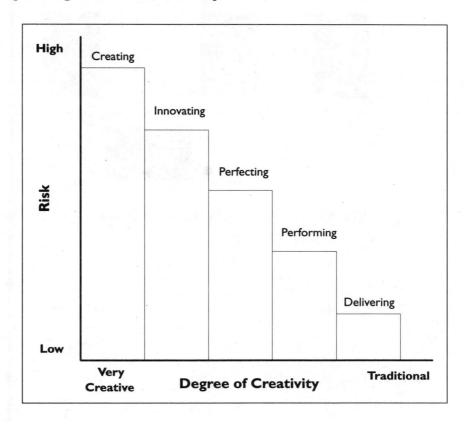

# Just for Fun

At the end of each chapter, we include a creativity-building exercise. Take a few minutes and devise a solution for each one as you encounter it. There is more than one solution for most of the exercises.

In this first exercise, draw a line from one box A to the other box A. Draw a line from one box B to the other box B. Draw a line from one box C to the other box C. You cannot cross any lines (either the lines you have drawn or the ones defining boxes), and you cannot go outside of the big box.

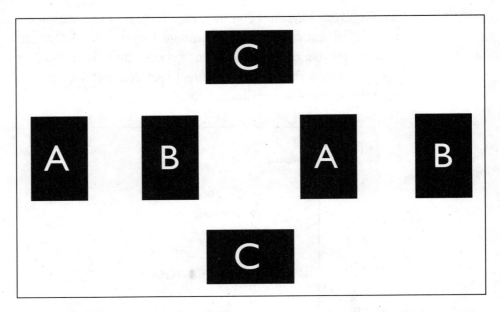

We have put one solution for this and every other Just-for-Fun opportunity in Appendix B. Enjoy!

# 2

# Letting Go:
# Waking Up Oscar

**W**e all have two personalities that live inside us. Think of them as Oscar and Felix of *The Odd Couple*. The Felix personality resides in the left hemisphere of the brain. Felix is a well-organized, highly literate individual who loves lists, plans everything he does, and never deviates from the plan. He is driven by rules and the clock. If rules do not exist, he develops them to define what is expected of him. He likes to have goals, either self-defined or set by others. He strives to please others and is very disappointed if others do not recognize his efforts.

Oscar, on the other hand, inhabits the right brain hemisphere, the creative side. Oscar's personality is unstructured, reactive, and driven by whims. For breakfast he drinks beer left open the night before. He challenges authority and rejects conformity. He feels best when he is working on many projects at the same time. He believes that rules are made to be broken. He marches to his own drummer and relies on self-gratification to keep him going.

Felix achieved a 4.0 grade average in college. He loved exams because they proved to his teachers that he had done his assignments and learned his lessons. Oscar squeaked by with a 2.0 average. He was a troublemaker in

**We all have an Oscar and a Felix inside our heads.**

class. He told jokes. He was more interested in making friends than in making grades. Felix works to accomplish something; Oscar does whatever he does for the joy of doing it.

We go to school and study to satisfy Felix's needs—to establish more rules, to define how things are done, and to lay out plans for attaining certain goals. From birth on, we are trained—first by our parents, then by our teachers, and later by our organizations—to conform to some predetermined norm. Felix is held up as the example of good and Oscar as the example of bad. Felix always wears a tie, has the correct time, knows from past experience or training what should be done next. Oscar—oh well, he is out to lunch.

Felix weaves rules and regulations into a creativity screen, so he can concentrate his efforts on getting the job done. The more new rules he can establish, the finer the mesh of the screen, and the more the creative thoughts can be filtered away from Felix's attention. The first step in increasing individual creativity is to start eliminating the rules that combine to screen out creative thoughts.

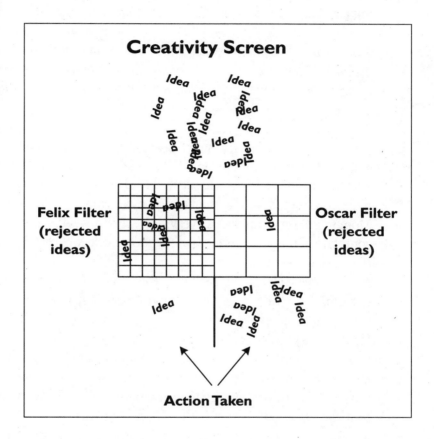

Things would work fine if either Oscar or Felix lived in the house (the mind) by himself, but this is not the case. As a result of the feedback we receive throughout our lives, we push the Oscar personality into the shadows, allowing it to emerge only when we relax. At night, when we sleep, Oscar rules with no interference from Felix because our sleeping thoughts do not normally result in action.

During the day, both Oscar and Felix live in the house and must therefore coexist. But Felix rules. Oscar functions like a child, reacting emotionally to outside circumstances. Because Oscar's outputs are radical and reactive,

Felix intervenes before we can put them into action. Felix takes Oscar's impulses and tries to put them in order, reshaping them according to Felix's rules for acceptable performance. This process often results in Felix's rejecting an idea and chastising Oscar for even suggesting it.

*Watch your thoughts; they become words. Watch your words; they become actions. Watch your actions; they become habits. Watch your habits; they become character. Watch your character; it becomes your destiny.*
FRANK OUTLAW

For instance, one morning Oscar suggests, "Smell the socks. If they don't smell too bad, put them on." Felix reacts in disgust: "No way! Rule 1593 states, 'Put clean socks on every day.' How dumb can you be?" Of course, Felix could wind up like the young boy at camp who'd been admonished by Mom to put on clean socks every day. After a week, the boy called Mom and complained that he couldn't get any more socks on! He followed the rules, but the results were not good.

In some cases, Felix reshapes the idea so drastically that Oscar cannot recognize it. After years of rejection, Oscar just gives up and stops submitting ideas, content to slip back into the shadow of the individual's dreams. Here is the problem that most of us face today: How do we get Felix to encourage Oscar to submit ideas? How do we get Felix to react to these ideas in a manner that Oscar will perceive as positive? How do we encourage the creative side of the personality to participate more actively in our day-to-day activities? That, simply put, is the objective of this book.

Everyone has three different thinking patterns: analytical, creative, and practical thinking.

You use the analytical thinking pattern when you make judgments and solve problems. This pattern rests in the left-hand side of the brain and is a "Felix" thinking pattern.

You use the creative thinking pattern when you are developing a way to do something that you have not done before and cannot rely on someone else's input to tell you what to do. This pattern, often used to develop new and clever solutions to situations, rests in the right-hand side of the brain. It is an "Oscar" thinking pattern.

You use the practical thinking pattern to help implement ideas that were developed by the two other thinking patterns. It is the ability to turn theory and concepts into accomplishments. This pattern, which rests in the left-hand side of the brain, is a "Felix" thinking pattern.

It is interesting to note that two of the three thinking patterns rest in the left-hand side of the brain. This feature makes it much easier for us to convert the ideas generated by the analytical thinking pattern to be accepted and implemented by the practical thinking pattern.

*Innovation Styles*
*Visioning: Looking for the ideal solution.*
*Modifying: Looking for ways to improve the current situation.*
*Experimenting: Looking for new information, with existing facts.*
*Exploring: Looking for ways to challenge existing assumptions.*
AUTHOR UNKNOWN

# Proactive Creativity

Far too often, people call on their creative powers only when faced with problems. This is truly unfortunate because they underutilize this gift by not applying it fully. As a result, they develop a reactive rather than a proactive approach to creation. We believe that people need to develop and use both reactive and proactive creative powers to make the most of their creative potential.

Different reasons drive individuals or groups to become creative. Following are the most common:

▶ Problem solving prompted by an event that is traumatic or emotionally significant. For example, you total your car and must create a new way to get to work.

▶ Playful brainstorming—listing new approaches to a routine situation—for example, serving a hotdog on a stick instead of in a bun.

▶ Systematic, purposeful creativity to fill a void or come up with a better way to do something. It need not be playful or aimed at problem solving.

> ▶ Satisfaction of a personal desire. Some people are driven to look at things in novel ways or feel a personal need to be creative.

To sharpen your creative powers, you need to establish a workout program and exercise your creative self at least three times a week. Individual workout sessions can vary from 5 to 60 minutes, depending on the exercises you select and your personal interest in the outcome. The idea of enclosing a CD/ROM in the back of this book was a product of one of these exercises.

## Setting the Stage for Creativity

 Creativity can show up anytime and anyplace. Sometimes we are very creative. At other times, it is simply impossible to pluck an original thought out of the brain. I've sat in front of my computer for hours, pecking at one key at a time to capture a few unimportant thoughts that I would only end up erasing. At other times, the ideas flow out of my mind so rapidly that they get lost because I cannot record them fast enough. We can do much to prepare ourselves to become more creative. We can position and train the Oscar side of the brain to speak out more often and the Felix side of the brain to listen more intently and openly to Oscar's ideas. To accomplish this, we need three conditions:

> ▶ **Time.** Extra time is often required to develop and sell a creative solution that is not in line with the individual's or the organization's culture.
>
> ▶ **Environment.** It is difficult to be truly creative when you are continuously interrupted with phone calls, questions, or children climbing on your lap.
>
> ▶ **Success.** Nothing gets Felix's attention better than receiving recognition for creative new solutions.

## The Creativity Work Space

Our emotions and actions are formed by our preconceived notions about the environment in which we find ourselves. When we enter a library, we talk softly and move carefully. When we go to a party, we laugh and smile more than usual. When we pick up a baby, we coo and gurgle as if we have no mind at all. When we go to the office, we become more conservative, reserved, and formal. When we go to a movie, we sit beside a friend for hours without talking—behavior that is not only acceptable but also expected. We have been trained from birth to conform to the expectations related to specific environments.

We like to set aside specific locations where we exercise our creativity. For Jim it is a desk in a small back bedroom. Before that, it was a credenza behind his desk at work. One of Bob and Glen's favorite places is a beach. They discovered this while conducting a class in Curaçao, where they spent each evening on the beach working on a new book. Your creativity spot need not be a grand place. It could be a workbench in the garage or an old desk in the cellar behind the furnace. The important thing is that in your mind, and in the minds of your family members or business associates, it is your space.

Associated with your space are specific rules:

RULE **1.**   No interruptions are tolerated except in case of emergency.

RULE **2.**   The clean desk policy does not apply. Do not take time to organize the work area, and declare it out-of-bounds to your family or your co-workers. Remember, Oscar's world is one of clutter and disorganization. Just think of the time you will save by not having to pick up, put away, and get out the same materials later.

RULE **3.**   Make your creativity place very visual. Use lots of adhesive notes. Jot good ideas on them and stick them up around your creativity area. Make sketches and flow diagrams, and post them on the walls as well. Put up varied, interesting pictures, and change them often. Your creativity place is for stimulating ideas, not impressing others.

RULE **4.**   Give yourself a relaxed atmosphere. Install an old, comfortable chair, one in which you can lean back and rest your head while your mind goes blank and opens to creative thoughts. Have furniture that you can put your feet on. Choose a spot that is not too hot or too cold.

**We all need our own creativity space.**

RULE 5.  Have the right equipment on hand. Be prepared to be flooded with new ideas. When they come, you need to be able to capture them rapidly. Here are some items that can be useful:
- ▶ Good lighting
- ▶ A computer
- ▶ Lots of paper
- ▶ Colored markers
- ▶ A tape recorder
- ▶ A CD or tape player (for restful music)

- ▶ A filing system
- ▶ A corkboard
- ▶ A bookcase
- ▶ A small copier

RULE **6.**  Have a focal point, something that relaxes you when you look at it. It could be a window that you look out of, or a small aquarium. Some people find that an ocean scene or an abstract painting does the job for them. Use whatever relaxes you.

Each person's creativity place is unique because it must fit with the individual's personality and output expectations. We are not saying that you must have such a place, but we strongly suggest considering it as a tool to help turn on your creative juices. Does having a creativity place mean that it is the only place where you will be creative? The answer is a resounding no. It is a lot like the jogging treadmill that you buy for training at home. When you get on the treadmill, you start to jog because the equipment is made specifically for that activity. But owning the treadmill does not prevent you from jogging around the neighborhood.

# Relax to Create

Often we find ourselves caught up in the stress and strain of everyday activities. Johnny gets hit in the head with a rock on the way to school. Johnson cancels the order. You realize that you forgot to send out the new schedule. Alice is sick, and no one knows what she did with the drawings. Your flight to Kent, Nebraska, has been canceled. How can you turn all these complications off and focus on being more creative when it takes all your energy and attention just to tread water and keep things going?

If the last paragraph describes your situation, it is best to start your creativity session with what a jogger would call stretching exercises. We call them calming or melt-down exercises. These are exercises designed to prepare the muscles you are about to use for the workout they are about to engage in. We use a number of these melt-down exercises, particularly meditation.

## Meditating to Create

Ever since the popularity of meditation exploded in the 1970s, devoted followers of all ages have not stopped praising its benefits and the way it revolutionized their lives. Countless testimonials describing decreased stress levels, increased energy, improved productivity, and heightened creativity have been recorded. For example, one study showed that people aged 40 and over who meditated 20 minutes twice daily had 74 percent fewer doctor visits and 69 percent fewer hospital admissions than the average population. Another study, involving employees of a New England bank and some northeastern industrial firms, revealed that meditators experienced fewer errors, less absenteeism, greater focus on work, and more creative ideas. Finally, researchers discovered that meditation helped business school students solve problems faster and develop more effective teamwork than their fellow students.

The demonstrated benefits are so compelling that many businesses, including the Adolph Coors Company, AT&T, New York Telephone Company, and Hoffman-La Roche, have incorporated meditation into their stress management programs. Johnson & Johnson reported that such programs enabled the company to hold its health care cost increase to 50 percent of the national average. Not only do structured meditation programs save money, they also give a company a competitive advantage by increasing employees' productivity and creativity.

In the midst of all the hype, many began to wonder what, exactly, meditation is. Skeptics resist it as a bizarre New Age religion. The subject can be confusing and easy to dismiss because there are so many meditation schools, approaches, and techniques. This complexity is compounded by technical jargon and notions of different meditative levels or states.

A universal characteristic of meditation is elevation to an altered state of consciousness brought about by clearing of the mind. Transcendental Meditation (TM) emerged as the prevalent meditation method after the Beatles publicly endorsed it. Founded by Maharishi Mahesh Yogi, TM can be learned only from teachers taught by the Maharishi himself. Throughout all 50 states are Maharishi Vedic Universities where learners can become initiated into the TM program. Following are some other meditation approaches:

▶ Clinically Standardized Meditation (CSM), developed by Dr. Patricia Carrington, author of the well-received *Freedom in Meditation*

▶ Respiratory One Method (ROM), developed by Dr. Herbert Benson, author of *The Relaxation Response*

▶ Self-hypnosis

You may ask, why should I meditate? The answers to that question converge on creativity. Our lives are so busy and hectic that most of us have many thoughts racing through our minds simultaneously. Meditating helps clear the mind of all those thoughts and relax so that it can focus on one thing at a time. Imagine your desktop strewn with piles of paper. If you add another report to the piles, it can easily get lost in the heap. Furthermore, you have trouble concentrating on that report—or anything else—because your thoughts stray over all the other work on your desk. By clearing the desk of all the clutter, you free yourself to focus on a single item.

Concentrating on one thing at a time helps the mind develop creative ideas. The most creative geniuses, such as Einstein and Mozart, sustained intense periods of absorption similar to the states achieved through meditation. An 8-year-old violinist at the Juilliard School of Music meditates to relax and become more expressive. We have all experienced such states of absorption—for example, watching a movie or listening to music so intently that we lose sight of our surroundings and the time. It is at such moments that our creative potential is the greatest.

Another powerful reason for meditating is that meditation alleviates stress. In the past, many thought that stress induced creativity; until recently, the debate over this issue remained unresolved. However, it is now widely accepted that the opposite is true. You will not grow less creative by eliminating stress. In fact, stress can sometimes inhibit creativity.

Try the following CSM exercise (read all six steps first):

STEP 1.    Go to a quiet place in your home, or close the door to your office.

STEP 2.    Sit upright in a chair with your hands in your lap and your feet flat on the floor. Sitting with your back perfectly straight will let you continue the exercise without getting tired.

STEP 3.    Close your eyes and relax all your muscles.

STEP **4.**   Focus on a calming word (mantra), phrase, or picture. For example, use the word *relax* or think of the ocean.

STEP **5.**   Repeat the mantra, and let it come and go through your mind. Do not try to force it.

STEP **6.**   Continue meditating for 10 to 20 minutes.

If you have not meditated before, it will be difficult to stay still for so long. You may even experience an uncontrollable itch or restlessness all over your body. But keep trying. It takes some time to build endurance for meditating.

In any bookstore or music store, you will find excellent cassette tapes that will help you relax and open your mind to new thought patterns. These tapes rely on subliminal learning and/or self-hypnosis. In one kind of tape, a moderator with a soft, melodic voice (like the feeling of velvet rubbed against the face) guides the listener on a vacation to a relaxing and quiet spot. Sensory words describe the place—for example, a patch of grass under a big tree beside a rippling stream, with the warm autumn sun shining down while billowy white clouds float lazily across the dark blue sky. The moderator encourages the listener to relax and enjoy the environment, feeling the rush of air in and out of the lungs. With each breath, the moderator encourages the the listener to exhale problems and pressures and breathe in uncontaminated fresh air. The object of such a tape is to enable the listener to enter into a relaxed state of mind by listening intently for about 10 minutes.

Another type of tape focuses on relaxing individual parts of the body until the whole is relaxed. The moderator may start by suggesting that you relax your jaw, then your eyes, shoulders, fingers, toes, and so on. Typically, the moderator will then have you focus on the peacefulness of your breathing, your body warmth, and the warm feeling you get when thinking about someone you love. Often, these tapes are complemented with soothing music or environmental sounds like waves breaking or raindrops falling. Still other tapes use music and environmental sounds as the primary message, which contains subliminal messages designed to relieve guilt and anger and reinforce feelings of confidence and self-fulfillment.

Two tapes that we particularly like are *Learning to Relax—Subliminal Motivation* by Dr. David Illig, published by Metacon Inc., and *Ten Minutes to*

*Relax,* based upon the book *Relaxation and Stress Reduction Workbook* by New Harbinger Publishing.

You may wonder about the time investment required for effective meditation. Typically, 10- to 15-minute sessions, three times a week, are adequate for most people, with additional sessions on particularly trying days. To begin, find a quiet spot where you will not be interrupted and can close your eyes for 10 to 30 minutes. Loosen your clothes before starting the tape.

Of course, meditation is not a panacea. Many have tried meditation with unsatisfying results. However, you will not know whether it is for you unless you try it first. Browse in your local bookstore or library for some of the many meditation books available. Ideal for the busy novice meditator, Salle Merrill Redfield's *The Joy of Meditating: A Beginner's Guide to the Art of Meditation* guides the reader through four brief meditation exercises. *Complete Meditation* by Steve Kravette is a thorough collection of exercises, with a specific one for creative inspiration and invention. *The New Three Minute Meditator* by David Harp takes a humorous approach, demystifying meditation; it is excellent for meditators at all levels. Even though many good books are available to guide the meditator, it is best to begin by finding a meditation class to attend. We have included in the accompanying CD/ROM a relaxing exercise entitled "Melting Your Cares Away" by Charles P. Mignosa. We believe you will find it very useful.

*The creative response usually happens in a state of relaxed attention.*
    ADELAIDE BRY

## Releasing Tension

As we become more and more tense, we rely more and more on the Felix side of the brain to respond to external and internal stimulations. Pressure, tension, worry, and anxiety erect a wall between Felix and Oscar that is often difficult to dismantle. We have found that one of the very best ways to break down this obstacle is by saturating it with sweat. Physical exercise improves our health—which includes the mind's health—thereby helping us to be more creative. You don't have to lift weights or do push-ups to increase your creative abilities. A lot of less strenuous physical exercises will increase your mental capabilities. We like the following approaches:

**Stretching.** Select exercises that stretch your cerebellum, motor cortex, and limbic system. There are a number of stretching positions that stimulate various portions of the body and brain. Targeting different areas of the brain helps relieve pent-up emotions.

**T'ai chi.** T'ai chi comprises a group of ancient Chinese physical exercises that can be performed by everyone from age 5 to 100 or more. Its slow, rhythmic motions bring the body and mind into complete harmony, reducing and, often, eliminating stress.

**Aerobics.** Medical research has demonstrated a direct relationship between cardiovascular health and brain function. Physical exercises like swimming, hiking, walking, dancing, and golf are excellent ways to develop a healthy mind and a creative spirit.

**Yoga.** Yoga is a longevity mind expander that uses body positions to induce brain wave patterns that increase blood flow to the brain, thereby improving its performance.

We recommend that you become familiar with each of these four types of brain expanders and experiment with them. Find out which approach, or combination of approaches, produces the best results for you. Once you've done this, you should design a physical mind expander program that uses your own optimum combination while rotating periodically to emphasize each of the four approaches. Individuals often find that one combination is very effective for a period of time and then another combination takes over. Continuous variation in physical mind expanders is important to a well-rounded program.

*If you choke off the silly ideas and only receive the good ones, the safe, can't miss ones, you might not get any ideas at all.*
MARSHALL J. COOK

We have introduced you to mind expanders designed to change the interface between the Felix and Oscar sides of your brain. We have shown you ways to relax, thereby helping you prepare to accommodate the creative powers that you already have, and we have provided you with mind expanders that will help you think differently. We strongly believe that

▶ When you enjoy being creative, you will seek out opportunities to be creative.

▶ When you enjoy what you are doing, you will be more creative.

The only person who can make you more creative is you!

## Just for Fun

Arrange the six matches so that each match touches every other match.

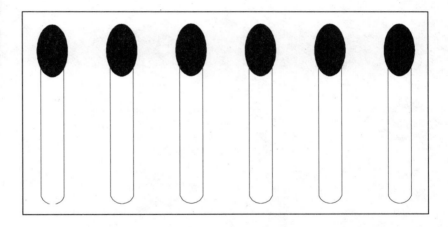

You can find an answer to this exercise in Appendix B.

# 3

# Harnessing Infinity: Developing Creative Focus

**C**reativity is the ability to come up with something that did not exist before. Creativity is designated by many terms such as *imagination, risk taking, independence of judgment, flexibility, curiosity, spontaneity,* and *perceptiveness.*

We have described the three key issues each of us faces in daily life: setting a direction, planning how to move in that direction, and completing the tasks that lead in that direction. Creativity is used at either the individual or the organizational level to address these three issues.

Individuals can be creative at both the personal and organizational levels, whereas groups normally exercise creativity only at the organizational level.

## Individual Level

As an individual, you can be creative in everything you do. Being creative can help you find easier and more effective ways of interacting with others and becoming more successful. A number of methodologies, tools, and techniques lend themselves to individual creativity. Being creative can be an individual experience.

Individual creativity is directed at finding solutions to personal problems, improving financial and/or living standards, and providing a level of personal satisfaction. Hobbies are often used as a way to attain personal creativity. It also relates to the approach an individual uses to complete a work assignment. In a development laboratory, personal creativity often results in patterns.

## Organizational Level.

An organization can be as simple as your family or as complex as a multinational corporation. It may be a business, an enterprise, a nonprofit group, or a government unit. Organizations need to be creative to provide increased value-added content to all of their stakeholders (stakeholders include management, investors, customers, suppliers, employees, the employees' families, and the community). Employees working harder can only provide a limited increased value-added content to the organization's stakeholders. Only through effective use of the creative powers of all of the organization's management, employees, and suppliers can the organization meet its obligations to increase its value to all stakeholders. Organizational creativity often is the result of a team working together on a situation.

People working together in groups often focus on being creative. Organizations normally stress group creativity. Group creativity can be at least as powerful as individual creativity, but it requires a somewhat different mindset. (Not everyone is good at both types of creativity; however, with effort and patience, we can all get better at both.) Groups take many forms—for example, natural work groups, families, cross-functional teams, process teams, project teams, ad hoc groups, and those on special projects or assignments. The methodology, tool, or technique that a group uses may depend on the nature of the group. Other factors in the choice include the expected outcome and the group's understanding of what creativity is and how to maximize it.

There are six different objectives to which creative activities can be directed (see the table). Tools play an important role in developing a creative individual or organization. There are many tools that can help you focus on each of these six objectives. Throughout the remainder of this book, we will

### The Six Different Creative Objectives

| | Impact Area | |
| --- | --- | --- |
| **Issues** | **Personal Impact** | **Organizational Impact** |
| Direction Setting | 1 | 4 |
| Planning | 2 | 5 |
| Doing | 3 | 6 |

introduce you to a number of creativity tools that will address each of these six objectives.

You have probably heard the familiar statement that creativity is 1 percent inspiration and 99 percent perspiration. This definition is a precursor to four styles of creativity that we have identified: structured creativity, nonlinear creativity, provoked creativity, and "Aha" creativity.

*The ultimate creative capacity of the brain may be, for practical purposes, infinite.*
Dr. W. Ross Adley

# Styles of Creativity

## Structured Creativity

The first style is the structured approach to creativity. It is used most frequently in organizations. One manifestation of this style is the linear model of problem identification, root cause analysis, breakthrough, and solution implementation.

Structured creativity can be described as

► Step by step,
► Detailed,
► Complex,
► Tool intensive,
► Tightly controlled,
► Requiring little facilitation, and
► Effective for individuals or groups.

Structured creativity is good for improving on tasks already being performed and for developing a set of tasks to implement a plan. It is usually focused on the day-to-day tasks of an individual or the operations of an organization. For example, if you find water on the kitchen floor, there must be a cause for the presence of that water. Following the linear model may lead you to understand that the sink leaks only when the dishwasher runs. This realization could lead you to find a clog in the dishwasher drainpipe. You replace the pipe, and the problem disappears.

## Nonlinear Creativity

The second style of creativity is represented in a methodology that occupies much space in current literature. It builds on open-ended thinking. Nonlinear creativity frees up human energy. Despite popular misconceptions, creativity does not require donning goofy hats and blowing horns. An example of nonlinear creativity is brainstorming, or generating ideas without concern about what they are connected to. Nonlinear creativity transcends rightness or wrongness.

Nonlinear creativity can be described as

▶ Exciting,
▶ Unpredictable,
▶ Fast paced,
▶ Focused on quantity, not quality,
▶ Promoting involvement of people, and
▶ Usually used in groups.

Nonlinear creativity is good for getting people involved. It promotes high energy and group ownership. It is best used for working on tasks that are understood and developing plans for new tasks. For example, nonlinear creativity is used in a brainstorming session to develop a new product for a company. Structured and nonlinear creativity are the styles of creativity most commonly seen in organizations.

## Provoked Creativity

The third style of creativity, provoked creativity, is rapidly gaining in popularity. Provoked creativity uses a catalyst of some sort to generate mental movement and develop new insights and understanding. The catalyst may be an analogy, a metaphor, a word chosen at random from the dictionary, a color, or some other tangential stimulus to evoke or create a new insight. Some people feel that this is the optimum style of creativity within a group. Common techniques include Six Hat Thinking, developed by Edward deBono, and TRIZ (also called TIPS or Systematic Innovation), developed by G. S. Altshuller.

Provoked creativity can be described as

▶ Catalyst focused,

▶ Providing a springboard for forward movement,

▶ Easy to build on,

▶ Easy to start,

▶ Requiring active facilitation, and

▶ Easily used by individuals or groups.

Provoked creativity is good for getting the creative juices flowing. It helps you address issues such as the context that you are in. It uses a mechanism such as a random word or scenario. Provoked creativity is very effective when you are working on developing plans and setting a direction, although it can also help with improving performance of activities. For example, when you start with a situation such as the leaking sink and then use a dictionary to find a word at random to spur your thinking along a different avenue than you would normally have taken, you have used a mechanism to provoke creative thought. It might lead you to install a garbage disposal to keep from developing future clogs in the drain.

## "Aha" Creativity

The fourth style of creativity is marked by the "Aha" or "Eureka" that is exclaimed (or felt) when a new, unconnected idea suddenly bursts forth. "Eureka"—"I found it" in Greek—is what Archimedes cried when he climbed into a bathtub and grasped the concept of displacement by volume. "Aha" has contributed the most to the major breakthroughs in the history of the planet, yet it is the least understood, the least studied, and the least practiced style of creativity. "Aha" creativity is the new idea that emerges from your ability to create that which did not exist before. It is the breakthrough that occurs when something truly new springs into the mind. Think, for example, of the paper clip: It began as a general conceptual breakthrough. Our experience has shown that "Aha" creativity produces fewer than 1 percent of all creative ideas.

"Aha" creativity can be described as

- ► Having no steps,
- ► Not containing patterns,
- ► Focusing on big issues,
- ► Frequently having one defining moment,
- ► Using simple methods, and
- ► Being individually intense.

Any style of creativity can help you work through each of the key issues of direction, planning, and doing, although certain styles are usually more effective with particular types of issues. In Chapters 5 through 13, we will show you tools for maximizing the effectiveness of each style.

## Approaches to Creativity

Creativity is a central ingredient in success for any individual or organization. Success means being effective in obtaining desired results, being efficient in doing an activity with minimum resources, being creative in establishing new and better methods, and being adaptive in responding to a changing environment.

Organizing for creativity should maximize the impact of the four different styles of creativity. To make the most of any creative effort, ask the following five questions:

- ► How are we going to proceed? In other words, which style are we going to use?
- ► Who is going to engage in the creative activity? Are we going to practice creativity individually or as a team? in a formal or an informal structure?
- ► What topic are we going to focus on? Against what challenge are we going to apply creative energies?

► When will this creativity be called on? Will we use it on demand? Will creativity become structured and formalized? Will there be scheduled meetings and agendas to follow?

► Where will the creativity be called on? Will it be used in the home or in the natural work area, or must we set aside some special place to make it happen?

*"Creativity is not a spectator sport."*
AUTHOR UNKNOWN

# Thinking Styles

Each person's primary frame of reference for creativity is his or her own individual makeup. Each individual has a unique way of processing and looking at things; this is his or her preferred thinking style.

Your thinking style has nothing to do with intelligence; rather it has to do with the span of time you are most comfortable envisioning. For instance, some people are able to conceptualize over broad time horizons and look at things in terms of decades or even centuries. Others prefer to think in years, months, and quarters. Events that occur in the latter frame of reference are those that require standards. The functional nature of all work implies a still more restricted time frame, with tasks being completed in a very localized area over days, hours, and minutes. Many individuals feel most comfortable thinking about these shorter time increments. To be successful, we must focus our creativity on the appropriate time event horizon.

Traditional organizational structures reflect this diversity in thinking styles. The top management of any organization should be most concerned with long-term thinking and expected outcomes. The analogy we use quite often is drawn from the 1991 hostilities in the Persian Gulf. General Norman Schwartzkopf set the direction, determining that the combined forces were going to do an end run through the desert and sneak up on Saddam Hussein's forces from the east.

The middle stratum of any organization is in charge of planning, allocating resources, and making sure that what happens is consistent with the thinking of the top stratum. People at this level develop the tactics that keep the organization on track. To extend our military analogy, it was the colonels, majors, and captains who developed plans to have the right troops and equipment in the correct positions so they could move quickly through the desert.

The stratum of the organization where most of the tasks are performed uses primarily short-term thinking. In the military, those performing at this level drive the tanks, fuel the trucks, and win the war.

None of these thinking styles is either good or bad; none is more or less valuable than another. Every organization, to be operative, requires a very large proportion of short-term task performance, thinking, and creativity. Few individuals in any organization engage in long-time-frame thinking.

We believe that these thinking styles form a continuum. It is not so much that one is distinctively different from another; rather, there is a rainbow blending from one to the next. It is not true that hourly workers perform all tasks and owners and senior executives do all direction setting. There are many seemingly minor tasks that the highest chief executive in the highest office must perform to fulfill his or her duties. Conversely, seemingly minor tasks require some long-term thinking.

The general nature of work is that repetitive work is done by the thousands and directional work by the half dozen. Your challenge is to understand how *you* can plan and organize for meaningful creativity.

Hundreds of tools are available to help you improve your creativity, individually or in groups. Each of the succeeding chapters will highlight some of our favorites. Many of these tools have several applications; however, we have classified them according to four styles (structured, nonlinear, provoked, and "Aha" creativity). Each style is described in more detail as it relates to individual thinking styles and organizational structure. Over the years, we have invented many of the tools in this book; you can invent your own. Feel free to create your own tools to fit the situations you are facing. Let us know how your efforts turn out.

*First comes thought, then organization of that thought into ideas and plans; the transformation of those plans into reality. The beginning, as you will observe, is in your imagination.*
NAPOLEON HILL

# Using Creativity in an Organization

The approach to creativity within an organization varies with the thinking style, the organizational stratum, and the key issue being addressed.

## Setting Direction

We start with the driving part of any organization, the top. At the top, it is critical to understand how the direction-setting creative activities are going to evolve. Some of these activities will come from the tool set that we are calling "Aha," for the style of creativity that calls forth something that did not previously exist. Tools in this set include things like taking a walk, questioning how something could be done using 10 percent of the resources, always having a blank piece of paper handy, or carrying a tape recorder. For instance, Brian Wilson of the Beach Boys had in his living room a sandbox with a piano in the middle. He used the unusual combination of playing in the sand and playing the piano in a free, unstructured approach to creating music.

This style of creativity requires empty rooms and open space. "Aha" creativity typically is an individual experience; it rarely occurs in groups or teams. Brian Wilson's assignment to himself was to create music and lyrics that had never existed before. He had no assignment to write a specific kind of music for a specific audience. Rather, he created the music that he wanted to create. When did he do it? His structure was completely random. His creative activity could occur at 2:00 A.M. or 2:00 P.M. "Aha" creativity is hard to plan, hard to schedule, and extremely hard to make happen on a schedule. It frequently occurs in a formatted workspace, a place that is conducive to this kind of innovative thinking. The space itself often determines the outcome of the effort. Your formatted workspace should be a place that allows your thoughts to mature and grow.

Thinkers at the top stratum of an organization also frequently rely on tools associated with provoked creativity, which uses some sort of catalyst to overcome inertia. Classical tools of provoked creativity enable you to surmount the block of the blank page, to deviate from your accustomed path. Provoked-creativity tools provide a license to change your approach by using toys or widgets, dictionary word searches, or any other catalyst to keep your mind alive and fresh.

Within an organization, provoked creativity is used in broad decisions about the configuration and allocation of resources. Typically, these decisions are rendered by teams that are their own bosses. For instance, a team may be a group of senior executives who must estimate how the market will evolve in the future. Their work is to develop the organization's direction and value system. In addition, they must identify the core competencies, the mission statements. This self-directed group is the only group of people positioned to work on the macro systems that define the organization. They must  be available to work on demand. For example, when Fred Smith, CEO of FedEx, decided to go into China, he was able to bring together his top managers, who decided how best to serve that part of the world. Their answer was to establish a major hub in the Philippines.

Major development of directions and systems requires an environment free of everyday pressures. The world contains many beautiful retreats, conference centers, golf courses, and other pleasant environments conducive to the provoking of creativity. Collectively, senior individuals and senior teams determine the direction and intent of an organization. Without creativity at this level, the organization will persist in doing what it has always done and will ultimately fail in today's rapidly changing marketplace. One challenge of any creative initiative in business is to support senior management by providing the environment, resources, and incentives to engage in provoked and "Aha" creativity using the appropriate tools.

Creativity is no less important for direction setting in individual lives. Each one of us must spend some time determining uniquely personal values and directions. The tools of provoked and "Aha" creativity can be as valuable to us in our personal lives as they are in organizations.

## Planning

Once we have set a direction, we need to work on the systems and processes that make it possible to move in that direction. (This is true for individuals as well as for organizations.) Work on systems and processes most frequently benefits from the tools of nonlinear and provoked creativity. The latter, discussed in the previous section, provoke movement against issues.

Ad hoc alliances are formed as needed in the real world of managers, engineers, and regional executives. Special groups are frequently constituted to deal with burning issues. These groups can work on systems and subsystems such as a purchasing process, an inventory maintenance process, an accounts payable process, and so forth. Quite often these creative initiatives involve special projects, reengineering, or process improvement. Many believe that nonlinear and provoked creativity occur on demand. They function best when there is an indication that systems are not working as well as they should—when systems are misconnected, customers dissatisfied, revenues lost, or resources wasted.

Groups using nonlinear or provoked creativity usually focus on systems redesign, process redesign, and project work. They tend to do their work in organizational conference rooms. Most large organizations have dedicated spaces with flip charts, breakout rooms, and so on, where people working on system and process design can retreat from the daily work environment.

The tools of nonlinear creativity will help a group to focus on a process or problem. The people involved are experts and will have a lot to say about the problem. It is important for them to feel comfortable, express themselves honestly and openly, and facilitate group creativity. Nonlinear tools encourage people to say what is on their minds. Just speaking up and collecting ideas that already exist in people's minds is a creative use of talents and ideas. Nonlinear tools enable people to gain insight into new ways of handling everyday problems.

## Doing

After an individual or an organization has established a system or a process that is functioning on a regular basis, the tools of structured and nonlinear creativity become appropriate. The most frequent users of structured creativity are not ad hoc groups but rather teams of people who work together under direction on an ongoing basis. Such groups can use structured and nonlinear tools to improve and error-proof processes and other assigned tasks.

Structured and nonlinear creativity usually follow a problem-solving model: For example, identify the problem, do a root cause analysis, make a breakthrough, develop a strategy, implement the strategy, and review to ensure progress.

Creativity tools can and should be used by everyone. However, they should be chosen carefully. In an organization there is a tremendous misconnection and loss of energy when the wrong style of creativity is applied to a specific problem, and participants naively expect their approach to have an impact on the direction of the organization.

Many believe that structured creativity can save them from themselves. True, the sergeant driving the vehicle across the desert may have some ideas about how to secure the vehicle at night, but that fact will not determine whether or not the army continues on to Baghdad. The overarching strategy of going around the Iraqis will not emerge from a group of sergeants out in the desert evaluating the issues facing them in tomorrow's battle.

## Summary

You should remember the following points:

- ▶ Using the tools for structured and nonlinear creativity will never produce the "Aha" style of creativity that most people assume they are looking for. Even using the tools from provoked creativity does not do that.
- ▶ Major "Aha" creativity does not follow a standard process or a set of rules. It comes from humans' innate ability to make new connections.
- ▶ Individuals, not tools, produce creativity; individuals, not teams, drive creativity. Generally, people who experience major "Ahas" have one or two such insights in their lifetimes. Those who have a large number of "Ahas" are a very, very small minority.

Individuals who are successful are those who can look ahead and see the long-term ramifications of their creative ideas and who also have the power and structure within their environments to move their ideas forward.

There are lots of tools to choose from. The difficulty in creativity is not the lack of tools but the lack of appropriate application of the tools.

- ▶ 80 percent of the creative breakthroughs are the result of 20 percent of the tools.
- ▶ You must pick the method that is correct for you.
- ▶ Creativity methodologies can be used in any order.
- ▶ Creative methods can be used more than once to address a given issue.
- ▶ Working on a given issue may indeed require several different approaches and methods.
- ▶ Simple methods are the best.
- ▶ Either group or individual efforts can be fruitful in achieving creativity. The determining factor is the context in which the method is being applied.
- ▶ This book has been designed so that you do not have to read it entirely to use its contexts.
- ▶ Each tool and method stands alone.

## Just for Fun

Which line is longer?

Appendix B contains our answer.

# 4

# Exercising Your Mind: Expanding Your Capability

## Introduction

Now it is time to exercise your creativity. This chapter will deal with simple, intermediate, and advanced mind expanders that are designed to unleash human creative powers. These exercises are not designed to solve problems or to create new concepts. They are designed to help you unleash your creative powers.

These mind expanders are designed to help you look at things in an entirely new light and develop an environment that will expand your ability to think more creatively. We will start out with a series of simple mind expanders that are endurance exercises, progress to some mind expanders of medium difficulty, and work up to some very complex ones by the end of the chapter.

*It was just an old block of stone sitting in the sun until Michelangelo walked by and saw David inside waiting to be released.*

H. JAMES HARRINGTON

# Simple Mind Expanders (SMEs)

## SME 1. The Two-Minute Mind

Sit in front of a clock or a watch that has a sweep second hand. Relax for a few moments, collect your attention, and when you are ready, direct your attention to the motion of the second hand. For two minutes, focus your awareness on the movement of the second hand as if nothing else in the universe existed. If you lose the thread of concentration by thinking of something else or just by spacing out, stop, collect your attention, and start again. Try to hold your concentration for two minutes.

## SME 2. Mindbeats

Slowly draw a pencil across a blank piece of paper. Concentrate on keeping your attention on the place where the pencil point becomes a line. Each time your mind wanders off, draw a mindbeat: mark the place with a kink in the line, as shown in the drawing. When you reach the edge of the paper, double back. How long can you keep an unbroken line of awareness?

**mindbeat** A means to develop a visual image that shows changes in concentration levels.

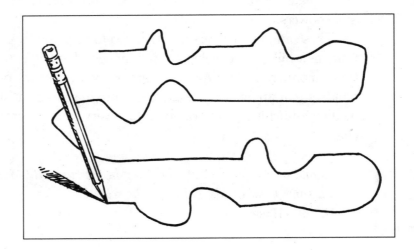

### SME 3. The Alphabet

In your head, count the number of capital letters of the alphabet that contain curved lines. Then count the number of small letters that contain straight lines.

### SME 4. The Numbers

Recite the ascending and descending series:
- ▶ Up by 2: 2, 4, 6, 8, . . . , 100; down by 2: 100, 98, 96, 94, . . . , 2
- ▶ Up by 3: 3, 6, 9, 12, . . . , 99; down by 3: 99, 96, 93, 90, . . . , 3

Do the same for all other numbers through 9.
Recite the double ascending series:
- ▶ Up by 2, 3: 2–3, 4–6, 6–9, 8–12, . . . , 66–99
- ▶ Down by 2, 3: 66–99, 64–96, 62–93, 60–90, . . . , 2–3

Do the same for other dual number combinations.
Do the same with triple ascending and descending combinations.

### SME 5. A Nursery Rhyme

Memorize the following verse:

Mary had a little lamb—
Its fleece was white as snow.
Everywhere that Mary went
The lamb was sure to go.

Recite the verse, numbering each word:

1 Mary 2 had 3 a 4 little 5 lamb—
6 Its 7 fleece 8 was 9 white 10 as 11 snow.
12 Everywhere 13 that 14 Mary 15 went
16 The 17 lamb 18 was 19 sure 20 to 21 go.

Recite the verse, preceding each word with the number of letters in the word:

4 Mary 3 had 1 a 6 little 4 lamb—
3 Its 6 fleece 3 was 5 white 2 as 4 snow.
10 Everywhere 4 that 4 Mary 4 went
3 The 4 lamb 3 was 4 sure 2 to 2 go.

## SME 6. Common Objects

Select two objects that are in your desk. Study them. Then write down two or three ways they could be changed to become more effective and useful. (In Chapter 7, you'll find a similar tool called "code talk" presented in greater detail.)

## SME 7. Personal Creativity

List two of your best creative ideas that have been implemented. Then list three things you personally can do to become more creative at work. Make another list of three things you personally can do to become more creative at home. (In Chapter 9, you'll find a similar tool called "five 'Why's'" presented in greater detail.)

Tom Wujec's book *Pumping Iron* contains many excellent exercises similar to these that will be quite a challenge. By now, you can see why these are called endurance exercises. We think you will also admit that they require a fair amount of concentration. Another source of concentration exercises is the newspaper; look for the puzzles and games usually included in the comics section. The Just for Fun exercises at the end of each chapter are also provided for this purpose.

# Medium-Difficulty Mind Expanders (MMEs)

## MME 1. Analyzing Outrageous Ideas

Keep a piece of paper with you. Every time you come up with an outrageous idea (Oscar's inputs) that you don't put to use, write it down. At the end of the day, review the list. Put check marks in front of the ideas that you now believe you should not have rejected. For each of the checked ideas, write down why you rejected it. Now select a sample (three to six) of the rejected ideas that you still believe are bad. List what was good about the "bad" ideas, what they would have accomplished, and why they were suggested. Then, focusing on each idea's good points, define how it could be reshaped to become an acceptable concept.

### Example.

While driving on the freeway, you change lanes and inadvertently cut off a driver who is speeding. The other driver may react by cutting over two lanes to pull up beside you, make an obscene gesture, and then speed up to get in front of you. Oscar immediately responds, telling Felix to speed up and box the other driver in, then slow down to keep that driver from moving forward in traffic. Felix quickly rejects the idea.

### Analysis.

What's good about the idea?
- ► It may slow down the fast driver.
- ► It may teach that driver not to use obscene gestures.
- ► It may make you feel good.

Why did Oscar suggest the idea?
- ► To get even with the other driver.

How can you change the idea to accomplish the desired results the next time the situation occurs?
- ► You can react to the obscene gesture by yelling out, "Sorry, my mistake. I'll be more careful next time."

This approach accomplishes almost everything that Oscar wanted to accomplish. It makes the other driver feel small and puts you in control. It also provides you with an appropriate reaction tool. (In Chapter 6, a similar tool called "cartoon drawing" is presented in greater detail.)

## MME 2. Pictures to Drive Creativity

We have all heard that a picture is worth a thousand words. Similarly, a picture can give rise to a thousand thoughts that can be combined into many creative ideas. Take the time to look at some magazines and cut out interesting pictures of a variety of people and situations. Choose pictures that stimulate thoughts and/or evoke ambiguities. Once you've collected a group of pictures, select three or four at random and create a story that includes the items in the pictures. (In Chapter 10, a similar tool called "drawing" is presented in greater detail.)

## MME 3. Words to Drive Creativity

Exercise MME 2 also works with words. Write interesting nouns on separate cards. Words that seem to work well are *apple, Monterey, Rio, sea, gum, tower, lighthouse, radio,* and the like. Pull three to five cards at random from

**Certain words will trigger creative responses.**

the pile, and make up a story using the nouns on those cards. In the motion picture *Leap of Faith,* Steve Martin played the part of a minister who led a traveling religious revival group. Their transportation broke down in a small town. To raise funds, the group put up their tent and held revival meetings. During one of these meetings, Steve Martin's character was challenged by his team to include in his sermon random words chosen by other team members. The resulting sermon was truly creative, as he included terms like *aluminum siding.* (In Chapter 9, a similar tool called "thinking words" is presented in greater detail.)

## MME 4. Differences and Similarities

Save the pile of cards you prepared in MME 3 after you have used them to develop stories. Shuffle the cards, and pull out two at random. Make a list of ways the two items are different. Make a second list of ways they are the same. For example, if you draw the words *car* and *house,* one easily noted difference is that the house is made of wood and the car is made of metal. Examples of similarities are that they both use electrical systems and that people enter both cars and houses. (In Chapter 8, a similar tool called "card sort" is presented in greater detail.)

## MME 5. Defining Other Applications

Here is another application of the pile of cards with key nouns written on them. Select a card at random. Ask yourself how the item named is normally used and in what other ways it could be used. For example, if you draw the term *coat hanger,* you will say that it is normally used to hang up clothes in a closet. Other potential atypical uses would be as a car antenna or an instrument to open a car door when you are locked out. How many different uses for a coat hanger can you come up with? We have had teams list over 75 different applications for a coat hanger. (In Chapter 5, a similar tool called "possibility generator" is presented in greater detail.)

*A creative idea is just an idea until something is done with it. You must do something or you are not creative.*
     GLEN HOFFHERR

## MME 6. Creative Progress Reports

At the end of each week, prepare a progress report on a three-by-five card. Take no more than five minutes to handwrite the report, which will be made up of four sections. On the top half of the front of the card, write what you did during the week. On the bottom half, write what you accomplished. Then turn the card over, and on the first line, record how you feel about your job (e.g., "excited," "unhappy," "bored," "challenged," "rushed," "overworked"). On the second line, record how you feel about what you accomplished (e.g., "nothing," "a job well done," "lots of fair output," "only finished 50 percent of the work I wanted to get done," "dissatisfied with the amount of output but pleased with its quality"). Use the rest of the card to record two ideas that would improve the way you feel about your job and your accomplishments. Then write a statement of what you will do the following week to make things better.

After you have made 10 weekly reports, review the 10 cards. Compile a list of all the suggested changes for improving the way you feel about your job and your accomplishments. Select the two most important suggestions, and prepare a plan to implement them within the next four weeks. Every month, update the list and define actions to correct the two most important conditions.

Each time you review your weekly progress report, evaluate whether you have implemented the weekly corrective action plan. Every month, calculate the percentage of weekly corrective actions that were successfully implemented. Keep a graph to plot the monthly percentages as shown.

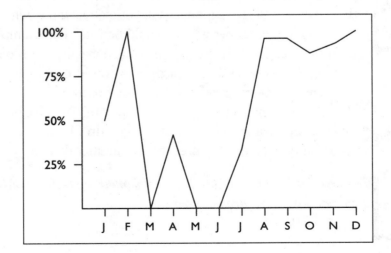

Also, review the trends related to your feelings each week, and plot them using a graph like the one shown. If your feelings have not improved, you need to question your weekly corrective actions. Don't expect other people to react to your problems if you haven't done everything you can to correct them first. (In Chapter 11, a similar tool called "presentation" is presented in greater detail.)

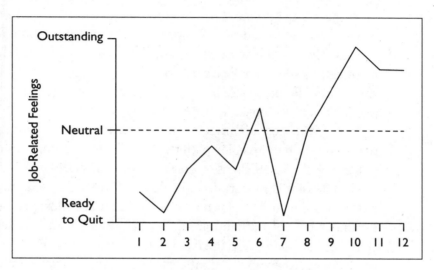

# Advanced Mind Expanders (AMEs)

## AME 1. Dreaming in Color

Most people dream in black and white. If you dream in color, you are one of the exceptional individuals who have high potential for creativity. Dreaming in black and white requires less activity on Oscar's part (the right brain); the result is that dreams have less impact upon the conscious being. Changing your dream pattern from black and white to color requires a little practice, but it is readily mastered by most people. This mind expander is designed to help you dream in color and increase the impact of your right brain on your conscious activities. You can almost think of it as the intensified impact of a movie when it is projected in Technicolor instead of in black and white.

To change your dream pattern, buy a selection of bright-colored sheets of letter-size paper from your local stationery store or copy shop. The colors should include bright red, yellow, green, blue, purple, and orange. Just before you go to bed, set aside five minutes to study one of the color chips intensely, without interruption. Then turn off the light, and for the next five minutes, try to visualize the color in your mind. Each night, repeat the cycle using a different color. As you repeat this mind expander, you will find that it becomes easier to visualize the color. After a short time, you will find that you can visualize a color without studying the color chip first. When this occurs, go directly to the visualization part of the exercise (selecting a different color each night). Some people have problems with certain colors and need to use particular color chips longer than others.

Once you become competent at visualizing the individual colors, you are ready to graduate to color patterns. Start with a simple pattern, maybe the pattern on a favorite dress or tie. Do not be concerned if you cannot visualize the exact color configuration; the object of the exercise is not to copy color patterns but to add a color dimension to thinking. Most people use this mind expander between 30 and 45 nights before experiencing the first "Technicolor" dream. Don't stop the five-minute pattern visualization with your first color dream. Keep up the nightly ritual until most of your dreams are in color. Then phase out the mind expander. You should expect to use this mind expander for about 45 to 60 days.

## AME 2. Recording Your Evening's Activities

Many good ideas occur while we are asleep. Creativity often explodes into the consciousness and is lost before it can be captured. We have all said to ourselves, "That was a great idea, but I can't remember what it was." As you increase your receptiveness to right-brain activities, these random explosions will happen more and more frequently. They will happen when you are driving to work, giving a presentation, talking to a friend, listening to a lecture, and very frequently, when you are asleep. It is very important to capture these flashes of brilliance when they occur because they quickly retrench to the subconscious again. When you wake up at night with an answer to a problem or a refinement to the way you are doing something, what options do you have?

1. Go back to sleep and hope that you remember the idea in the morning.
2. Stay awake the rest of the night so that you won't forget it.
3. Record the concept so that you can return to your restful sleep without worry.

Of course, the correct answer is number 3. Keep a pad and pencil beside your bed to record great and even not-so great ideas that come to you during the night. I have recently abandoned pages and pencil in favor of a small dictating scratch pad at my wife's request to stop turning on the light and waking her up during the night.

Don't limit this practice to the bedroom. At all times, keep a means available to record the exploding ideas. Whenever an explosion occurs, record it right away. Also record what you are doing when the idea occurs (playing golf, watching TV, attending a meeting, etc.). Keep a graph that records the number of creative ideas you have each week. Set a target to double the number over a two-month period. Also analyze this information to determine in which environments you are most creative. Use the information to create environments that increase your creativity potential.

## AME 3. Discarding the Boombox

Most good songwriters can create music mentally without the aid of instruments. In truth, most people have the same creative power but do not take the time to develop it. Another very effective mind expander is one that will help you emulate the songwriters. When you have mastered this exercise, you will be able mentally to recreate music that you have heard—and at a higher quality level than the best stereo can produce. In addition, you will be able to orchestrate songs to complement your moods. You will be able to bring up the violins, highlight the flutes, or call for a clarinet solo. The combinations are endless. You can mentally have Frank Sinatra sing "I've Been Working on the Railroad" accompanied by Judy Garland. But first, you have to internalize the music.

To start this mind expander, select a song or a group of songs with rich instrumental accompaniments. We use the following Richard Rodgers songs:

▶ "Bewitched, Bothered, and Bewildered"
▶ "I Didn't Know What Time It Was"

▶ "If I Loved You"
▶ "Where or When"
▶ "Manhattan"
▶ "Some Enchanted Evening"
▶ "I Enjoy Being a Girl"
▶ "Oklahoma"

Now set up your stereo to play the same combination of songs over and over for a minimum of 30 minutes a day. Do this for a two-week period. We like to listen as we travel to and from work.

Next, make a tape on which you record every other song, leaving blank spaces on the tape for the songs that are missing. For example, record "Bewitched, Bothered, and Bewildered." Don't record "I Didn't Know What Time It Was," but leave the tape blank for that song's exact play time. Then record "If I Loved You." Then leave the tape blank for the exact play time for "Where or When." Then record "Manhattan," and so on. After playing the full tape over and over for two to four weeks, you will find that you automatically create the music in your own mind without concentrating on it. Now, use the tape with the blank sections to see if you can recreate the missing music.

The recorded sections stimulate your mind to prepare itself for the blank part of the tape that you will fill in mentally. If your mind has not been preconditioned adequately to fill in the blank spots, go back to the complete tape for an additional week. Once you have conditioned yourself to fill in the missing songs, try mentally creating the entire song sequence without the aid of a tape.

When you have developed the ability to create the set of songs, try varying the arrangements by calling for instrumental solos and/or adding more brass to the orchestration. Some people have trouble with this part of the mind expander and need to listen to tapes featuring different types of instruments before they can vary the instrumentation mentally. Once you have mastered this technique for one set of songs, you will find that you can apply it to any other song after hearing it just a few times.

You are now ready to add voice to the music. Select a singer whom you particularly like. Listen over and over again to that person singing the same set of songs so that you become very familiar with his or her timing and emphasis. Now, try to hear in your mind how the vocalist would sound if he or she sang one of the songs you used in the first part of this mind expander (for example, Doris Day singing "Some Enchanted Evening"). When you are successful, repeat the experiment with another vocalist who has a very different technique. Listen to the new vocalist singing a set of songs until you can mentally project the second vocalist singing the chosen song. For example, think how Willie Nelson would render "Some Enchanted Evening." You will find that you can quickly expand your voice vocabulary and even create duets as you master the technique.

This mind expander will enable you to create many hours of enjoyment for yourself. We particularly like to use it on airplanes to pass the many hours of otherwise boring flights. Unfortunately, this mind expander cannot replace your boombox completely. Because the technique requires a great deal of concentration, it will not provide background music when you are engaged in another activity. Also, you will need your boombox to introduce new music to your personal repertoire. (In Chapter 7, we describe another use of music, called "song titles.")

To foster creative efforts, it is critical to break established patterns. The mind expanders that we have introduced are designed to change your thought patterns. We have not tried to present mind expanders aimed at problem solving because we feel that the first requirement in freeing up your creativity abilities is to get enjoyment from being creative. We strongly believe that

- ▶ It is critical to expand the way you think.
- ▶ You need to practice thinking creatively on a daily basis.
- ▶ You can become more creative if you try.

No one can force you to become more creative—you must want to do it. Practice can help. Just using your mind in a consistent way can help you become consistently creative. You can expand your mind, but it takes practice.

## Just for Fun

A tree farmer planted 36 trees in nice straight rows. Unfortunately, deer ate 16 of his trees. The farmer decided to erect a fence around each of the remaining trees. He constructed six straight fences, each of which ran from one edge of the field to another. Each tree was fenced by itself, although some fenced areas contained the stumps of trees that had been lost. How did the farmer do it?

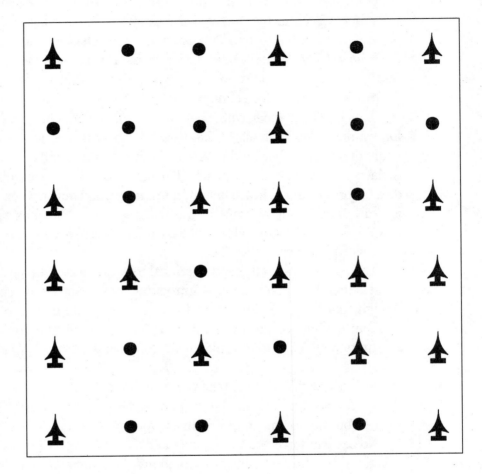

See Appendix B for an answer.

*Whether you think you can or whether you think you can't, you're right.*
    HENRY FORD

*There's a way to do it better—find it.*
    THOMAS A. EDISON

CHAPTER | **5**

# Setting Direction: Understanding Your Context

**N**either individuals nor organizations suffer from a lack of creative ideas. However, both suffer from the lack of successful application of those creative ideas. The true value of new ideas is realized when they are put into action. Putting ideas into action is not easy. Because people and organizations lack ways of sorting good ideas from bad ideas or practical ideas from impractical ideas, the ideas often die without being implemented.

Creative success lies in the application of a creative idea, which is bounded by its frame of reference. Suppose, for example, that you create a design for remodeling your kitchen. Your idea may be great and the design beautiful, but your creative ideas will only be apparent if they are implemented. To determine your frame of reference, you need to answer certain questions: Do you plan to move in the next year? Do you like to remodel? Can you afford to have the remodeling done now?

This chapter presents unique methods for establishing a context within which to answer the overall question, Are we being creative within our frame of reference? We call the four methods the selection window; the possibility generator; exaggerating objectives; and the manager to manager event. Each uses a different style of creativity—structured, nonlinear, provoked, or "Aha."

Setting your direction requires the ability to look into the future and determine a vector, a course of action, that will get you where you need to go. In organizations, these direction-setting decisions are typically in the hands of senior executives or those in the top management stratum. On a personal level, we are our own senior executives and managers and must set our own directions. A fascinating method for determining that direction and communicating it is what we call a manager to manager event.

We also examine a technique called the possibility generator for creating a large number of new ideas in a very short time. The possibility generator concentrates on the quantity of ideas, not on their quality; it frees our minds to create relationships at a very rapid rate. When an abundance of new ideas is available, a simple sorting method, the selection window, focuses our creative ability on determining where to invest time and energy. It is a powerful yet simple tool for identifying which new ideas to pursue.

A fixed objective allows everyone in the organization to see where we are going. Exaggerating objectives, or overstating a position, is a method that allows us to stretch our creative abilities in a very specific way.

*An executive woke up one day to discover that it was 15 degrees outside, snowing, and windy. She prayed for the strength to get up, get dressed, and jog 10 miles. Then she rolled over and went back to sleep. Instead of strength, she had received wisdom.*

UNKNOWN

Throughout the remainder of the book, we will introduce a number of tools. Because the Felix in us requires some order, each tool will be presented in a similar fashion. We will begin with a "creativity cue card" that shows the name of the tool, its type, the issue it's best for, whether it functions best for an individual or a group, and its basic steps. We will proceed by describing each step of the tool and giving an example that illustrates its use. We will provide a variety of examples from business and personal situations. Each example is only a starting point. Every tool presented can be used in more than one way, for more than one reason. Be creative in your selection and use of these tools—that is what they are for.

*The greatest trouble with most of us is that our demands upon ourselves are so feeble, the call upon the great so weak and intermittent that it makes no impression upon the creative energies; it lacks the force that transmutes desires into realities.*

ORISON SWETT MARDEN

## Selection Window

### SELECTION WINDOW

**Type:** Structured
**Issue:** Doing
**Who:** Individual

**Step 1.** Develop a list of ideas.

**Step 2.** Give each idea a score for each criterion.

**Step 3.** Place the ideas into the selection window.

**Step 4.** Analyze and do.

The selection window is a technique to help you select the right things to do. It uses two criteria, effort (resources) and probability of success, and provides a way to prioritize a list of options against those criteria. Using this tool enables you to consider each option systematically.

Begin by generating a list of options, alternatives, or opportunities that can help you see where you might apply your creativity. (You may choose to use one of the tools found elsewhere in this book, such as brainstorming, mind mapping, and brainwriting.) It helps to number each option. Draw a window containing four equal panes or boxes. Draw a scale of 1 to 10 (low to high) on the left and bottom sides of the window. Label the left side "Probability" and the bottom side "Effort." Evaluate each option on your list against the criteria of effort and probability of success. Ask, "How much effort will it take to accomplish this?" and "How likely is it that this idea will succeed?" Give a score between 1 and 10 to each answer. Place the number of the option at the point in the window where the two answer points intersect. When you have plotted answers for all your options on the window graph, you can review the selection window and take appropriate action.

## Example: Using Selection Window

### Step 1. Develop a list of ideas.

What can you do to help your friend who has AIDS?

1. Change nothing.
2. Never see the person again.
3. Call the person every day or every week.
4. Participate in an AIDS walk.
5. Develop a cure for AIDS.
6. Walk your friend's dog for him or her.
7. Shop for groceries for your friend.

### Step 2. Give each idea a score for each criterion.

| | Probability of Success | Effort |
|---|---|---|
| 1. Change nothing. | 6 | 2 |
| 2. Never see the person again. | 1 | 2 |
| 3. Call the person every day or every week. | 8 | 4 |
| 4. Participate in an AIDS walk. | 3 | 7 |
| 5. Develop a cure for AIDS. | 1 | 10 |
| 6. Walk your friend's dog for him or her. | 6 | 9 |
| 7. Shop for groceries for your friend. | 5 | 6 |

## Step 3. Plot the scores for your ideas in the selection window.

## Step 4. Analyze and act.

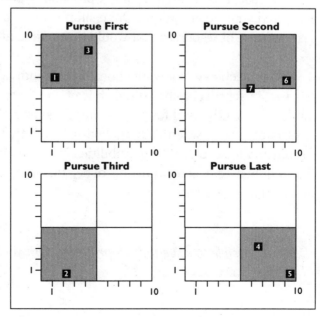

**Pursue First**  First, pursue items with high probability of success and low cost in effort. These are the "right" things that you feel will work best. Each could have significant impact and would mean only a small drain on your resources.

**Pursue Second**  For items associated with high probability of success and high effort, it is often beneficial to enlist the help of others. Those items are important enough to deserve the attention of a skilled group of people truly working together.

**Pursue Third**  Place items of low probability and low effort on a to-do list. Use these items as fillers. Although they have low probability of success, they are important enough to justify a modest expenditure of resources. Be careful! The line between items for immediate attention and those on the to-do list often gets blurred. The to-do items often dominate our time, to the exclusion of the more important items.

**Pursue Last**  Postpone items of low probability and high effort until you have explored your other options. Quite simply, the end does not justify the great expenditure of resources that would be required at this time.

The selection window functions best for individuals working on personal issues. It uses a very structured style of creativity. It is best applied to tasks and is frequently used for prioritizing to-do lists. The creative power of this tool is best seen when it is applied to items that encompass a short time frame and to sort a list of possibilities in a structured way. Because creativity requires that something be done, this tool helps you prioritize what should be done first.

*It is not possible to solve today's problems with yesterday's solutions.*
ROGER VON OECH

# Exaggerated Objectives

| **CUE CARD** | **EXAGGERATED OBJECTIVES** |

**EXAGGERATED OBJECTIVES**

**Type:** Nonlinear
**Issue:** Direction
**Who:** Group

**Step 1.** Define the opportunity.

**Step 2.** List the criteria that will satisfy the opportunity.

**Step 3.** Exaggerate the criteria.

**Step 4.** Use the exaggerated criteria to generate ideas.

By exaggerating objectives, individuals often can break through the cultural barriers that they have unconsciously erected. Exaggeration provides different perspectives to enable you to approach an opportunity creatively. To use this technique, start by listing the major objectives or criteria that your creative solution should satisfy. Then stretch each criterion in some fashion. There is no single way to do this. You may enlarge the criterion, shrink it, or change its limits. Use the exaggerated criteria to stimulate creative ideas.

## Example: Exaggerated Objectives

### Step 1. Define the opportunity.

▶ Increase involvement of parents in their children's education.

### Step 2. List the criteria that will satisfy the opportunity.

▶ Each child spends at least two hours per week working with his or her parents on things related to education.
▶ Parents know what their children are learning.

### Step 3. Exaggerate the criteria.

▶ Parents attend classes with their children on a regular basis.

▶ Children cannot pass any standardized test.

### Step 4. Use the exaggerated criteria to generate ideas.

▶ Pay for a college education for every high school student who has one parent attend all classes with him or her.

▶ Provide home computers for children who achieve better than a specified score on a standardized test.

Exaggerating objectives functions best for groups working on issues that face enterprises. It uses nonlinear creativity. It is best applied in direction setting. The creative power of this tool is best seen when it is applied to time frames of months or even years. It provides a way for an organization to stretch and break out of its normal modes of thinking. This tool helps you understand where you want to go.

## Possibility Generator

## POSSIBILITY GENERATOR

**Type:** Provoked

**Issue:** Planning

**Who:** Group

**Step 1.** Define objective.

**Step 2.** Break each element into subelements.

**Step 3.** Combine subelements into any new ideas that come to mind.

**Step 4.** Evaluate new options using the Selection Window tool to decide which to pursue.

The possibility generator is a method for stimulating ideas in a systematic way. Apply this tool to opportunities that encompass many potential elements. Begin by writing the opportunity or objective at the top of a page. Then identify its basic elements, and break those elements into their component subelements. Combine the subelements to suggest different ideas; try not to make value judgments at this time. Refine the ideas. You might want to use the selection window to prioritize the ideas using criteria that are important to you.

## Example: Using Possibility Generator

### Step 1. Define the objective.

► Develop new modes of transportation.

### Step 2. Identify the elements, and break each element into subelements.

| Types | Kinds | Functions |
|---|---|---|
| 1 Public | 1 Car | 1 Move people |
| 2 Private | 2 Truck | 2 Deliver freight |
| 3 In building | 3 Train | 3 Fun |
| 4 Outdoors | 4 Limousine | 4 Skiing |
| 5 Special needs | 5 Van | 5 Cross rough |
| | 6 Animal | terrain |
| | 7 Elevator | |

### Step 3. Combine subelements into any new ideas that come to mind.

It works best to choose one subelement from each list. Using dice or some other method for randomizing numbers helps to break your normal thought patterns.

► Suppose that your numbers are 4, 6, and 4. You have the following combination:

| Type | 4 | Outdoors |
|---|---|---|
| Kind | 6 | Animal |
| Function | 4 | Skiing |

▶ One possible mode of transportation using that combination would be a dog sled hauling skiers to the top of a ski slope.

**Using a possibility generator helps you come up with solutions you may never have considered.**

▶ Suppose that you generate random numbers again and get 3, 7, and 2:

| | | |
|---|---|---|
| Type | 3 | In building |
| Kind | 7 | Elevator |
| Function | 2 | Deliver freight |

▶ A possible mode of transportation would be an elevator that lifts trucks to the points where the freight is needed.

**Step 4. Using the selection window, evaluate your new options to help you to decide which you should pursue.**

The possibility generator functions best for groups working on issues that face enterprises. It uses provoked creativity. It is best applied to the development of plans. The creative power of this tool is best seen when it is applied to time frames of months and even years. It is a way for an organization to change its approach to what it does. This tool helps you understand how you can get to where you want to go.

# Manager to Manager Event

## MANAGER TO MANAGER EVENT

**Type:**  "Aha"
**Issue:**  Direction
**Who:**  Group

**Step 1.**  Hold work unit workshop.

**Step 2.**  Have unit manager's management sit behind unit manager.

**Step 3.**  Unit presents recommendations.

**Step 4.**  Manager makes yes/no or specific date decision.

The manager to manager event is a special type of presentation that follows a workshop held to address pressing issues. The workshop centers on the work unit; the participants focus on identifying opportunities or problems and developing recommendations. Near the end of the workshop, the unit makes a presentation to the unit manager. During the presentation, the unit manager's manager sits behind the unit manager. For each recommendation, the unit manager must make a decision: yes, no, or defer the decision to a specific date (yes and no decisions are encouraged). This method can be very stressful because the unit manager cannot see his or her superior's reactions to the decisions. However, this approach enables people to address a number of opportunities quickly.

The manager to manager event functions best for groups working on issues that face enterprises. It calls on "Aha" creativity. It is best applied to large issues that affect the direction of the organization. The creative power of this tool is best seen when it is applied to time frames of months and even years. It is a way to cause individuals within organizations to change their beliefs and open new lines of communication.

Direction setting is as important for individuals as it is for organizations. The direction one sets provides a constant reference for decisions throughout one's lifetime. Successfully applying creativity requires a well-defined set of values as well as an understanding of what you are trying to accomplish and your frame of reference.

- ▶ Core values and purpose differ from individual to individual and organization to organization. Both are needed to help you set your direction.
- ▶ Core values last a lifetime. They should survive and transcend the ups and downs of daily life.
- ▶ Your core values must be broad enough to allow for experimentation, failure, growth, and change.
- ▶ Your direction needs to work for you, not for someone else. A shared vision may not work for everyone in the organization; some people in an organization may not be happy or comfortable with it. The common vision must work for the organization.
- ▶ Setting direction does not imply or define specific day-to-day tasks and planning.

This chapter has presented tools with which to build on your core values and create and articulate your direction. These tools help either an individual or an organization answer questions such as Where do we want to go? What is the visible vector we are establishing for ourselves? What do we value? What is our purpose—what are we all about? These tools can help you be more creative and follow your direction.

## Just for Fun

Are these circles the same size?

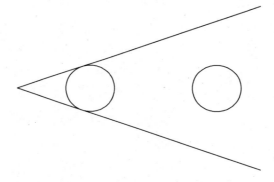

The answer is in Appendix B if you need to look.

# 6

# Suspending Rules: Gaining New Insights

In many situations, we must suspend the normal rules of behavior to be able to communicate more effectively. Often, an organization has an environment in which a no-talk rule seems to prevail. For example, in a recent visit to one organization, we had an opportunity to chat with a staff member (let's call her Liz) who mentioned that her hobby was bike riding and that she planned to take a 250-mile bike trip during an upcoming vacation. We happened to comment to Liz's boss that the planned bike trip sounded like an interesting way to spend a vacation. The boss responded that she didn't know that Liz was a biker and that biking was her own hobby. We discussed the fact that Liz had worked for her boss for over 12 years and yet the boss had no real information about who she was, about her needs and feelings. This lack of information typifies the work environment where information exchange is at a minimum.

Having encountered this situation so many times, we have been trying to determine its cause. When we interviewed some managers on this issue, they gave a common response: "I don't want to get to know my people because I may have to fire them, and if I know them, it will be more difficult to let them go."

We have devised a scale for assessing communication. You can listen to the conversations around you and find where on the scale most of them belong. At the lowest level in the negative zone is slander, where one person sets out to tell falsehoods about another, to hurt that person, denigrate him or her, make him or her look bad. Many individuals who suffer from feelings of inferiority or low self-esteem need to run others down to make themselves feel strong and healthy.

The second level of conversation is the exchange of lies and untruths. People engage in such conversation not necessarily to denigrate others but just to present a distorted view of reality, so they can make themselves look good, make their points, or win the day. These negative communications extend to misdirection—intentional omission of helpful information, withholding of information that could be conducive to a new and better environment. The existence of such negative communications leads to some bizarre rules in organizations. One place we visited has a reason for dismissal called "malicious obedience," defined as follows: If a supervisor tells a worker to do something that the worker knows is wrong, and the worker follows orders and damage results, the worker can be fired.

That organization attempted to develop a rule that would make people function at a higher level than robots. Many organizations, in contrast, have implied no-talk rules ensuring that people come to work and perform their tasks, do nothing outside their cubicles, and go home at night. In such an organization, the employee is not an individual, just a human servo-mechanism. A notch above no talking is dealing in small talk: "Do you think it will snow?" "The president's doing a good job." "Looks like the Hawks may have a winning season." The next higher level of communication, beyond the mere exchange of pleasantries during the day, is the exchange of hard facts, of realities: "What is going on?" "We mailed out 35 invoices yesterday." "We grossed $65,000 this month." "Overtime is up 16 percent." This endless array of facts is mind-numbing.

At a higher level of communication, people feel free to express their opinions. "You know, I think we would be a lot better off if we developed a system for optical scanning of bar codes; that would help us maintain our inventory." "I would like to see less overtime. In my opinion, we would be more profitable if we were to limit overtime." The authors have observed the following communication hierarchy; the top and bottom boundaries are not fixed but seem to be expanding.

Needs
Feelings
Options
Facts
Clichés
No talk
Misdirection
Manipulation
Malice

The trust that is required to move up the hierarchy is found in a culture or an environment where it is okay occasionally to make a mistake. Such an environment provides the liberty to learn. It frees people to express their feelings, their true opinions: "Well, I don't particularly like carrots." "I don't think green looks good on those walls." When there is true, honest, and open exchange of information, people can articulate their needs—what we need to have happen in this relationship, in this environment, in this organization, in this department. For creativity to grow, we must often suspend for a while the old rules of misdirection, lies, and slander to create a communication environment that allows us to be open and honest and express true needs and feelings.

*A new idea is delicate. It can be killed by a sneer or a yawn; it can be stabbed to death by a quip, and worried to death by a frown on the right man's brow.*
CHARLIE BROWNER

A minimal amount of rule suspension frees us to see situations from different points of view. In this chapter, we will discuss a technique called say/think that shows the difference between what we say and what we think. We also will explore the use of role-play scenarios to gain insight into current or future situations from unusual or unique points of view. A third technique,

cartoon drawing, presents situations as comic strips and requires participants to develop the dialogue in the balloons. The chapter will conclude with
a focus on listening for comprehension.

## Say/Think

**CUE CARD**

# SAY/THINK

**Type:** Structured
**Issue:** Doing
**Who:** Group

**Step 1.** Draw three columns on a pad.

**Step 2.** Record what is said in a conversation and by whom it was said.

**Step 3.** Write down what you were thinking after each state-ment.

**Step 4.** Review what was said and what you thought. If you trust the person(s) with whom you had the conversation, share your written thoughts.

The say/think method is a very simple form of linguistic analysis. It facilitates an individual's understanding of someone else. Groups can also use it to
understand each other's positions or the position of a higher authority. The
say/think method can help you in personal and business relationships. Simply prepare a piece of paper with three columns. You write down what is actually said in the first column, who said it in the second column, and what
you were thinking in the third. There are two ways to analyze the results. The
easiest way is simply to review the conversation alone, reanalyzing what was
said and what you thought. For a much more effective analysis, you can com-

pare and discuss your note sheet with the sheets of the others who were involved. If you want more information, add a column to record what you felt whenever something was said.

# Example: Using Say/Think

## Step 1. Draw three columns on a pad.

| Who | What Was Said | What I Thought |
|-----|---------------|----------------|
|     |               |                |

## Step 2. Record what is said in a conversation and by whom it was said.

## Step 3. Write down what you were thinking after each statement.

▶ This is Mary's record.

| Who | What Was Said | What I Thought |
|-----|---------------|----------------|
| Mary | Do you remember that tonight we have been dating for three months? | I wonder if he feels trapped into our relationship. He's not saying anything. I wonder if he feels trapped in our relationship. |
| Mary | Is everything all right? | He's upset! What can I do or say? I don't want to lose him. |
| Glen | No, everything is OK. I just forgot something. | He wants to propose and he forgot the ring. |
| Mary | Oh! | Oh Wow! |

▶ This is Glen's record.

| Who | What Was Said | What I Thought |
|-----|---------------|----------------|
| Mary | Do you remember that tonight we have been dating for three months? | Gosh has it been that long. That means the warranty on my new engine is about to expire. |
| Mary | Is everything all right? | I keep hearing that engine knock. |
| Glen | No, everything is OK. I just forgot something. | I need to take my car back to the shop before the warranty expires. |
| Mary | Oh! | Oh #@%&! |

## Step 4. Review what was said and what you thought. If you trust the person(s) with whom you had the conversation, share your written thoughts.

Sharing their writings, Mary and Glen produced significant surprises for each other. After analyzing this conversation, they were able to open up to each other and share their real feelings. They were married six months later.

Say/think is a tool that functions best for groups working on personal issues. It uses a very structured style of creativity. It can easily be applied to direction setting, planning, and tasks. The creative power of this tool is best seen when it is applied to short time frames—for instance, in examining in a structured way what has just been said. This tool provides a very powerful way to manage differences and unleash creativity focused on consensus.

*Behold the turtle; he makes progress only when he sticks his neck out.*
JAMES BRYANT CONANT

# Role-Playing

**CUE CARD**

## ROLE-PLAYING

**Type:** Nonlinear
**Issue:** Doing
**Who:** Group

**Step 1.** Define the opportunity, problem, or situation.

**Step 2.** Define who is or should be involved.

**Step 3.** Assign a role to each individual.

**Step 4.** Role-play.

**Step 5.** Debrief, focusing on new insights and learnings.

Role-playing is a way to examine a situation from many different points of view. It is most effective when it involves more than one person and when it is used to examine a real opportunity, problem, or situation. Each participant assumes the role of someone involved in a situation—such as the customer, service representative, salesperson, or executive—and portrays the situation from the assigned perspective. Role-playing can help people anticipate or improve opportunities, problems, or situations.

*A lack of questions presupposes assumptions, and that is foolish.*
   HIPPOLYTOS

## Example: Using Role-Playing

### Step 1. Define the opportunity, problem, or situation.

▶ We are about to launch our new MAGLEV product.

### Step 2. Define who is or should be involved.

▶ Representatives from Research and Development, Manufacturing, Shipping, and Sales; customer.

### Step 3. Assign a role to each individual.

▶ A representative from each department is participating in the role-playing session. Assign a role to each person; ensure that participants play roles other than their real-life ones. (The vice-president of marketing will play the customer.)

### Step 4. Role-play.

▶ The customer starts the role-play with the statement, "I want my MAGLEV delivered next week. It has been on order for three months." The salesperson responds, "Oh, that will be no problem." The salesperson then makes an immediate call to shipping and asks, "Has XYZ Company's MAGLEV been shipped yet?" Shipping's response is "It was scheduled to ship last week." Shipping calls manufacturing and demands, "When will the first MAGLEV be completed so we can ship it?" Manufacturing responds, "We cannot build this thing until R&D completes the design. They say that it should be done next month. After that we will still need to develop our manufacturing process."

### Step 5. Debrief, focusing on new insights and learnings.

This simple role-play yields a number of insights. The customer will be very upset if he or she is not informed of the delay. There is a communication problem between shipping and sales. Manufacturing is not ready to build the product. The product does not have a stable design.

Role-playing is a tool that functions best for groups working on enterprise issues. It uses a very nonlinear style of creativity. It is best applied to tasks. The creative power of this tool is best seen when it is applied to short time frames. It provides a structured way to look behind what is actually said and to examine from different perspectives what is happening.

# Cartoon Drawing

# CARTOON DRAWING

**Type:**  Provoked
**Issue:**  Planning
**Who:**  Individual

**Step 1.**  Define the opportunity, problem, or situation.

**Step 2.**  Use an existing cartoon with the words or titles removed, or draw a new cartoon that seems to capture something about the opportunity, problem, or situation.

**Step 3.**  Develop new captions.

**Step 4.**  Debrief, focusing on new insights and learnings.

Using cartoons as a stimulus allows you to suspend the rules that dominate your normal reality. The use of humor injects a different perspective as you look at the way things actually work in your world. If you cannot draw, use a cartoon from any source, and remove the words and titles. Give the cartoon to those involved, and have them develop their own words and titles.

## Example: Using Cartoon Drawing

### Step 1. Define the opportunity, problem, or situation.

► What is creativity?

### Step 2. Use an existing cartoon with the words and titles removed, or draw a new cartoon figure that seems to capture something about the opportunity, problem, or situation.

### Step 3. Develop new captions.

### Step 4. Debrief, focusing on new insights and learnings.

► The thinker may need to get a pad. Creativity can come from anyone at any time. If you look only for "Aha" creativity, you may miss many chances to be creative.

Cartoon drawing is a tool that functions best for individuals working on personal issues. It uses provoked creativity. It is best applied to both planning and tasks. The creative power of this tool is best seen when it is applied to short and moderate time frames. It provides a way to examine germane issues creatively in a nonthreatening situation, to examine what is happening from different perspectives.

## Listening for Comprehension

### LISTENING FOR COMPREHENSION

**Type:** "Aha"
**Issue:** Direction
**Who:** Individual

**Step 1.** Hear all the words spoken by someone.

**Step 2.** Seek the logic behind the words.

**Step 3.** Determine the motivation behind the logic.

**Step 4.** Understand the feelings about the logic.

**Step 5.** Frame your understanding in your own words.

Listening is a vital prerequisite to the ability to communicate with others. If we do not listen for comprehension, we miss data, misunderstand others' motives, and promote distrust. To listen for comprehension, you must seek understanding. You must hear all the words that are spoken. You must seek the logic inherent in the words. Beyond the logic, you must determine the motivation which is driven by feelings. When you understand another person's words at this level, it is important to frame the understanding in your own words.

Listening for comprehension requires that your listening be active, attentive, reflective, empathetic, and searching. Listening for comprehension allows you to grow in your understanding of others and prepare them to hear and understand you.

Listening for comprehension functions best for individuals working on personal issues. It uses "Aha" creativity. It is best applied to direction setting. The creative power of this tool is seen when it is applied to any time frame. It provides a way to examine and understand what is being said and to examine what is understood by those you deal with.

Suspending the rules is very difficult to do because we often do not even recognize that we are following rules in our thinking. The rules are often unstated and pervade the culture. Honest communication is meaningless unless it is heard. Sometimes we need to stop sending out information and simply receive and process the information coming at us. This chapter has presented four of the many methods that are available to help promote open and honest communication. Say/Think is a concrete method for demonstrating the distance between what we feel and what we say. Role-playing is a technique for putting energies into different points of view. Cartoon drawing is a fun, simple, and straightforward way to create new insights. Listening for comprehension is a very serious attempt to overcome the double talk that is present in most relationships when people do not say what they think and do not believe what they say.

Suspending the rules that we normally apply to a situation often frees us to become more creative. Tapping into many different individual views of a situation requires the ability to

- ▶ Suspend the rules that normally limit our thinking.
- ▶ Listen carefully to what others are saying.
- ▶ Assume positions that we normally would not take.

The tools presented in this chapter allow people to take on different roles or points of view as they address issues. The key to role-playing is the ability to listen. As individuals we are weak at listening, and listening is a crucial aspect of communication. Communication, in turn, is one of the most overlooked keys to implementing creative ideas.

# Just for Fun

Are the horizontal lines the same length?

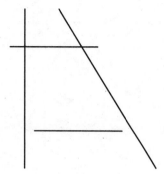

The answer is found in Appendix B.

# 7

# Thinking Differently: Shattering Paradigms

**P**eople, systems, and organizations are as they are because they are as they are. That may sound obvious, but most people do not understand that the status quo in any situation is nothing more complicated than the balancing of a set of forces. We have defined creativity as coming up with something that did not exist before. To create a new status quo—a new relationship, a new insight, a new set of systems, or a new process—we must disrupt the status quo. Ideas must be allowed to flow freely. We as individuals must think in new and creative ways. We need to give ourselves a license to think—to quote James Bond, "A license to talk, a license to listen." Many environments are by their very nature toxic. Toxic organizations, situations, and families inhibit or destroy the creative process. Chapter 3 presented several straightforward methods for developing a new vocabulary or a new way to exchange ideas. In some environments, the level of toxicity is so high that ordinary conversations are not possible. In those situations, people must find other ways to effect communication, such as writing a letter, creating a video, or using a computer to express what the situation really is.

People often feel safer and more creative when they look at an issue from an imagined point of view. It is often helpful to label the situation we are in with the title of a song, a TV show, or a movie. An open forum for brainstorming is an accessible method for generating numerous ideas. Using metaphors is a way of approaching a situation via something that is familiar. Free association helps us transcend the boundaries that normally keep us from moving forward. These methodologies unleash the fundamental power behind each individual's creativity.

## Song Titles

**CUE CARD**

### SONG TITLES

**Type:**  Structured
**Issue:**  Direction
**Who:**  Individual

**Step 1.**  Define the opportunity, problem, or situation.

**Step 2.**  Think of an appropriate song, TV show, or movie title that describes the situation.

**Step 3.**  Explain why the song, TV show, or movie title is appropriate.

Think of a title that fits your situation; then explain why you have chosen that particular title.

### Example: Using Song Titles

**Step 1. Define the opportunity, problem, or situation.**

▶ The government agency that I work for is participating in a "reinventing government" project.

**Step 2. Think of an appropriate song, TV show, or movie title that describes the situation.**

▶ "It's a Mad, Mad, Mad, Mad World."

**Step 3. Explain why the song, TV show, or movie title is appropriate.**

▶ We have always performed our jobs the way we currently perform them. If there were a better way to do them, we would be using it already.

Using song, movie, or TV show titles functions best for individuals working on enterprise issues. It uses very structured creativity. It is best applied to direction setting. The creative power of this tool is best seen when it is applied to long time frames. It provides a quick and accurate view of the values that are most important. This tool is excellent for sharing individual values with groups.

# Brainstorming

| **BRAINSTORMING** | |
|---|---|
| **Type:** | Nonlinear |
| **Issue:** | Doing |
| **Who:** | Group |
| **Step 1.** | Select a purpose for this brainstorming session. Be as specific as possible, but consider the resources available to the group. |
| **Step 2.** | Review the rules of brainstorming. |
| **Step 3.** | Generate ideas. |

Brainstorming is a way to generate a large number of ideas in a short time. It can help break existing thought patterns and facilitate the generation of new options. Brainstorming encourages strange, wild, or fanciful ideas. All ideas are valuable; do not judge or evaluate them. The goal of brainstorming is to create as many ideas as possible. Even the most unrealistic idea can provide the stimulus or basis for a totally new and valuable one. Having many new ideas increases the possibility of generating an excellent solution. Build on ideas. Join two or more ideas into still another idea.

*Creative Thinkers:*
*Are discontent with the status quo.*
*Seek alternative solutions to problems or opportunities.*
*Are alert to things around them that may trigger ideas.*
*Turn a negative into a positive by viewing it from different angles.*
*Work hard at it.*
  DAVID TANNER

## Example: Using Brainstorming

**Step 1. Select a purpose for the brainstorming session. Be as specific as possible, but consider the resources available to the group.**

▶ We need to improve our education system.

**Step 2. Review the rules of brainstorming.**

▶ The rules of brainstorming are explained in the next section of this chapter.

**Step 3. Generate ideas.**

▶ Pay teachers more money.
▶ Do away with tenure.
▶ Only teach students who want to learn.
▶ Keep everyone a student until he or she reaches age 21.
▶ Run the school as a business.
▶ Set national standards for students.

- ▶ Only use experienced individuals as teachers.
- ▶ Hire more administrators.
- ▶ Fire all administrators.

As you can see, some of the ideas on the list are mutually exclusive. That is okay because at this point, you are just soliciting any and all ideas. Later, you will have to do something with the list. For example, you might use a selection window to sort the ideas according to your evaluation criteria. That next step, not the brainstorming session, is the time for judgment.

# Brainstorming Variations

Over the years, a number of variations on brainstorming have surfaced. Virtually all variations in current use focus on the amount of prework and structure applied to the process. Prework is the preparation made before the start of the group session for generating ideas. It can be elaborate or minimal. Structure refers to the way the session itself is conducted. As with prework, there is a broad continuum of structures that can be applied to brainstorming. The minimum structure is the requirement to interact with others and follow some basic rules in a free-for-all session. In the most structured approach, participants take turns in a predetermined order, with each one required to provide an idea or say "Pass."

## Rules of Brainstorming

- ▶ Defer judgment. Do not permit criticism or evaluation at this time. Withhold discussion and evaluation of ideas until later.
- ▶ Freewheel. The wilder the idea, the better; it is easier to tame down than to think up. Even though an idea may seem ridiculous, it may be just the one that triggers a highly innovative, usable idea.
- ▶ Seek quantity. The greater the number of ideas, the greater the likelihood of producing winning ideas. The way to have a good idea is to have many ideas.
- ▶ Piggyback/hitchhike. Combine and discuss improvements. Build on ideas. Move ideas forward. Join two or more ideas into still another idea.

▶ Record ideas on a flip chart. Ideas are fleeting. Don't lose them! Record all ideas where participants can see them easily.

▶ Introduce competition. When possible, encourage competition between groups and/or challenge participants to meet or exceed a quota. This will stimulate creativity and the generation of wild ideas.

▶ Use active listening responses. Encourage responses by smiling, nodding, and making eye contact with participants.

Brainstorming is a method that functions best for groups working on enterprise issues. It uses nonlinear creativity. It is best applied to tasks. The creative power of this tool is best seen when it is applied to short time frames. It is a quick and accessible method for stimulating many ideas. This tool is great for energizing groups. It is vital to keep brainstorming sessions focused.

## Code Talk

**CODE TALK**

**Type:** Provoked
**Issue:** Planning
**Who:** Group

**Step 1.** Describe the opportunity, problem, or situation.

**Step 2.** Develop a different way to describe the opportunity, problem, or situation, such as in terms of a garden, a zoo, or a circus.

**Step 3.** Analyze your description for new insights.

**Step 4.** Develop more than one solution based on your new insights.

When you creatively connect two dissimilar thoughts, new solutions emerge. You may choose to emphasize the similarities or differences between things. By building on unusual perspectives, you produce creative ideas. Using code to talk about a situation enables you to analyze it in terms of something else. For instance, you may say that there are too many elephants in the circus, when you really mean that you have too many copy machines.

## Example: Using Code Talk

### Step 1. Describe the opportunity, problem, or situation.

► We must get people to notice our direct mail advertisements.

**Here the executive thinks in the code of a desktop battle ground.**

### Step 2. Develop several different ways to describe the opportunity, problem, or situation.

► Mailroom maze
► Desktop battleground
► Catch their eye
► Advertising jungle

### Step 3. Analyze the descriptions for new insights.

▶ Individuals in large organizations may not have mail delivered to them if it is not first class. Desktops are often cluttered, so the advertisements must stand out. Every individual receives many advertisements in a day.

### Step 4. Develop more than one solution based on your descriptions.

▶ Send advertisements disguised as business letters or in priority mail envelopes.

▶ Use electronic mail as a medium for advertising.

Code talk is a method that functions best for groups working on enterprise issues. It uses provoked creativity. It is best applied to planning. The creative power of this tool is best seen when it is applied to medium time frames. It is a powerful method for evoking new ways of looking at current practices. This tool is excellent for uncovering problems. It is often convenient to use a zoo, a circus, or a garden as a frame of reference.

## Free Association

**CUE CARD**

# FREE ASSOCIATION

**Type:** "Aha"
**Issue:** Planning
**Who:** Individual

**Step 1.** Get out of your normal environment.

**Step 2.** Pick any word, idea, or concept.

**Step 3.** Freely associate this idea with something else.

**Step 4.** Continue to build on the ideas as they come until you have exhausted your possibilities or you have experienced an "Aha."

Free association is a method for making mental connections between two different ideas. It provides a simple way to examine things that are similar, that are opposites, or that have a physical relationship. For instance, similar items might be a flower and a tree (both are growing things). A pair of opposites might be summer and winter. Items that share a physical relationship might be Paris and the Eiffel Tower.

Free association works best for a group of people with no specific end in mind. It is a very powerful tool for developing "Aha" ideas.

## Example: Using Free Association

The Campbell Soup Company used free association to develop the concept of Campbell's Chunky Soups. A development group began with the word *handle,* which led them through several other concepts, such as tools and utensils. Someone suggested a fork as a utensil, and one of the developers was prompted to joke about eating soup with a fork. The joke led to a discussion of how to accomplish that action, and the discussion directly resulted in the development of a very thick soup.

Free association usually requires the linking of 12 to 15 ideas before a useful idea results. Write your ideas down as they occur, or you will forget them. Some people prefer to use a tape or video recorder instead.

Free association is a method that functions best for individuals working on personal issues. It calls on "Aha" creativity. It is best applied to direction setting. The creative power of this tool is best seen when it is applied to long time frames. It is a method for stimulating chains of ideas.

Thinking differently gives us new, rich, powerful ways to look at opportunities, problems, and situations. Using the methods described here helps us break down the traditional walls and barriers that we have created and allows us to channel our creativity in new ways. The premise of thinking differently is to approach a situation without the normal constraints of our work environment. Using these methods enables us to channel our energies into creative, new, and exciting insights. Thinking differently facilitates looking at the current situation and removing some of the inhibitors and fears that block truly creative thinking.

# Just for Fun

Are the diagonal lines parallel?

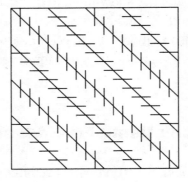

You can find the answer in Appendix B.

# 8

# Establishing Formatted Work Spaces: Unleashing the Value of Surroundings

**T**here are three parts to every job. The first is deciding what the task is; the second is planning how to carry out the task; the third is carrying out the task. Whether we are looking at a large organization—in which these tasks are largely assigned to different departments, different people, or different subgroups—or a sole proprietorship with one employee, all three parts must be addressed.

We must decide what we are going to do, plan how we will go about doing it, and indeed actually perform the task. At the very basic level, to take the example of meal planning, someone first must decide what we are going to have for dinner ("It would be nice today to have pork chops, apple sauce, and baked potatoes"). Someone has to plan the menu, buy the ingredients, cook the food, and serve the meal. There is a lot more to preparing a pork chop dinner than just cooking pork chops. There is a lot more to any job than simply performing the task.

To be creative, we must allow time and energy not only for task work—doing the job—but also for planning work (deciding how we will do it) and directional work (deciding what we will do). This special kind of work, thinking and creating, requires a particular fertile environment, which we call a formatted work space.

The formatted work space is becoming more and more a part of every organization. Every issue of *Fortune, Forbes, Success,* or *Inc.* magazine seems to contain articles on the virtual office or the virtual organization—people working at home via the Internet or other technologies that are available to create formatted work spaces on demand in new and innovative ways. For anyone with appropriate hardware and software anywhere on the planet Earth, the Internet provides a World Wide Web for cruising and sharing ideas 24 hours a day, seven days a week, 365 days a year. Formatted thinking work spaces are created and dissolved electronically from microsecond to microsecond around the world.

The trend is just beginning; we have barely touched the power of applied technology. The challenge, however, is not the acquisition of this technology; rather, it is the application of technology to the creation of formatted work spaces that will foster creativity in your life, in your organization. This chapter presents four helpful methods for working in formatted work spaces: force analysis, card sort, mind mapping, and environment.

# Force Analysis

## FORCE ANALYSIS

**Type:**   Structured
**Issue:**   Doing
**Who:**   Group

**Step 1.**   Define your opportunity, problem, or situation.

**Step 2.**   Draw a large circle.

**Step 3.**   Describe what is preventing you from succeeding (restraining forces).

**Step 4.**   Define or describe why you need to succeed (driving forces).

**Step 5.**   Analyze each of the forces.

Force analysis is a technique for making conflicting forces visible. It provides a way to visualize growth forces versus restraining forces and to map internal forces versus external forces. This technique can help you discipline your thinking and identify the keys to success.

*We must all become innovators to keep up with our volatile and exciting times.*
TOM PETERS

## Example: Using Force Analysis

### Step 1. Define your opportunity, problem, or situation.

▶ Sales are declining.

### Step 2. Draw a large circle.

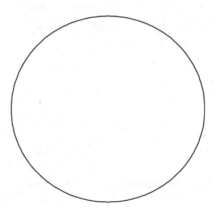

### Step 3. Define or describe what is preventing you from succeeding (restraining forces).

To represent each restraining force, draw an arrow outside the circle, pointing toward the center. The length of the arrows should indicate the strength of each force that is working against you.

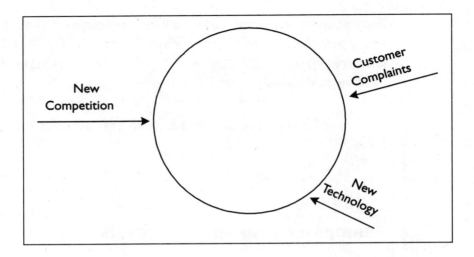

### Step 4. Define or describe your motivations to succeed (driving forces).

Identify anything at your disposal that can motivate or energize you to succeed. For each item, draw an arrow inside the circle, pointing away from the center. The length of the arrows should indicate the strength of each driving force. Continue identifying and marking the driving and restraining forces until you run out of ideas.

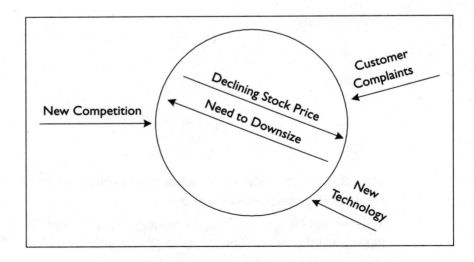

**Step 5. Analyze each of the forces, and consider the following questions:**

- ▶ Is there a driving force that can overcome each resisting force?
- ▶ Can you reduce the resisting forces?
- ▶ Can you increase the driving forces by strengthening them or adding new ones?

In the preceding example, the driving and resisting forces do not seem to be matched up very well. There seems to be an overriding mandate from management to downsize and to drive up market value. However, this strategy may not work in light of increased competition and customer dissatisfaction.

Force analysis is a method that functions best for groups working on enterprise issues. It uses a very structured style of creativity. It is best applied to tasks. The creative power of this tool is best seen when it is applied to short time frames. It provides a quick and accurate view of what is driving and what is resisting your efforts.

# Card Sort/Affinity Diagram

**CUE CARD**

## CARD SORT/AFFINITY DIAGRAM

**Type:** Nonlinear
**Issue:** Planning
**Who:** Group

**Step 1.** Define your opportunity, problem, or situation in very broad terms. Word the definition carefully.

**Step 2.** Generate ideas using brainstorming.

**Step 3.** Sort the idea cards into groups.

**Step 4.** Generate header cards.

Originally this tool was called card sort; today, however, it is most commonly known as the affinity diagram. It is an effective way to stimulate creativity in a group. It can also help provide structure for a large number of ideas. This technique works well with sensitive topics because it promotes interaction without criticism. The affinity diagram is a synergistic tool that can help you to break through barriers that might have impeded progress in the past.

## Example: Using Card Sort/Affinity Diagram

**Step 1. Define the opportunity, problem, or situation in very broad terms. Word the definition clearly.**

▶ Decide what needs to be covered in a book on creativity.

**Step 2. Generate ideas using brainstorming. Each idea should be expressed in at least three words, including a noun and a verb.**

Write each idea on a separate card. Place only one idea on a card, and write clearly so all participants can read the cards.

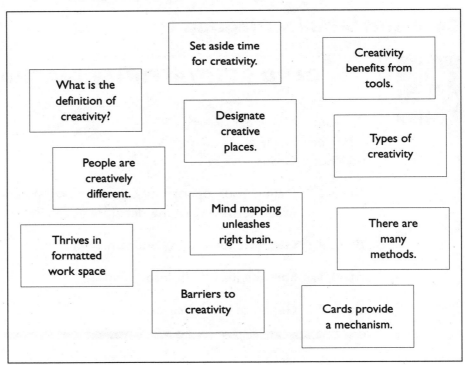

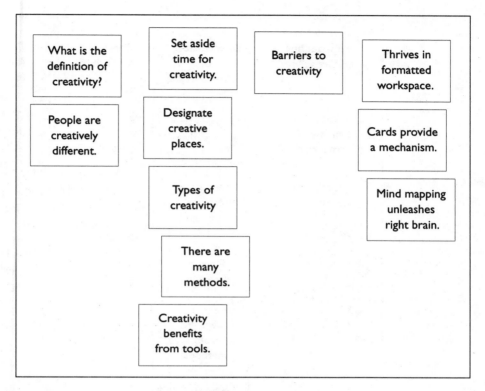

## Step 3. Sort the idea cards into groups.

Everyone must sort the cards at the same time. Sort in silence. Sort the cards by placing a card next to another card to which you feel it is related or with which it has something in common. You may move a card that someone else has positioned. Continue sorting in silence until the sorting visibly slows down. This normally takes about 15 to 20 minutes.

## Step 4. Generate header cards.

Discussion is encouraged during this step. For each group of cards, generate a header that captures the essence of all the ideas on the cards. Each header statement needs at least three words, including a noun and a verb. Make headers as specific as possible. Write them on cards, and place them above the cards in the appropriate categories. (You may choose an idea card as a header.) Mark header cards to distinguish them from the idea cards. Mark all the other cards in the category with a letter or number to identity them with the header.

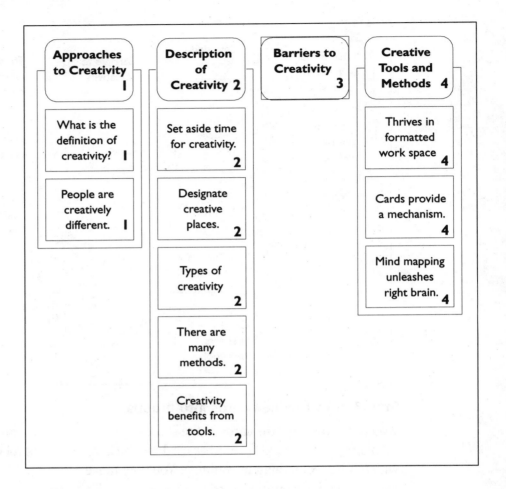

Card sort/affinity diagram functions best for groups working on enterprise issues. It uses nonlinear creativity. It is best applied to planning. The creative power of this tool is best seen when it is applied to medium time frames. It is a powerful method for removing the politics of developing ideas because everyone has equal power.

*It's too bad that thinking is not a required course in public schools. Not remembering, but thinking.*

EARL NIGHTINGALE

# Mind Mapping

**CUE CARD**

## MIND MAPPING

**Type:** Provoked
**Issue:** Planning
**Who:** Individual

**Step 1.** Define the topic.

**Step 2.** Draw a central image of the topic.

**Step 3.** Record related images around the central image.

**Step 4.** Repeat the technique for each of the new images.

**Step 5.** Expand images as long as your creativity continues.

**Step 6.** Group together ideas that have common themes.

Mind mapping is a creativity technique that integrates the processing of the whole brain. It promotes the visualization of ideas and provides a method to expand creativity by balancing the influence of logical evaluation with free-wheeling concepts and ideas. Mind mapping is very effective in helping you break through old paradigms using the intuitive powers of the mind. Because this technique is both visual and logical, it aids in the generation of creative alternatives. Mind mapping uses color and images to invoke the right brain and to break word-oriented left-brain tendencies. Selected use of words integrates the left brain into the mind-mapping process.

One or two individuals usually complete mind maps, but they can incorporate the creativity ability of many people working together if the formatted work space is structured appropriately. Groups can work on the same map on a chart pad or board or build new images from the images of others. Mind mapping is also useful for taking notes or outlining a book.

# Example: Using Mind Mapping

### Step 1. Define the topic.

The topic can be a goal to be accomplished or a problem to be solved.

▶ We need to develop an outline for a book on creativity.

### Step 2. Draw a central image of the topic. Use color and a symbol to involve the creative right brain.

Place the image roughly in the center of the work area. You may place a word or two next to the central image if that helps you to focus.

### Step 3. Record related images around the central image.

Don't worry about your drawing ability; just capture the images that come to mind. You may need to put a single word next to an image. Try to avoid using words, but if the creative process is being held up, use a word and continue. The more images you employ, the greater will be your right-brain involvement. This activity is the truly creative part of mind mapping. A formatted work space that is quiet or has relaxing music can further stimulate your creativity. Connect each of the new images to the central image with a line.

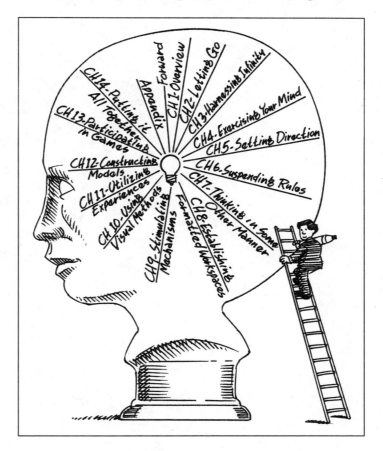

### Step 4. Repeat the technique for each of the new images.

From each image, let your mind wander just as you did with the central image. As other images come to mind, record them around the image from which they were generated. When you are through generating images, connect each image to its related image. Remember, a single word can be used as an image if no visual image will come to mind.

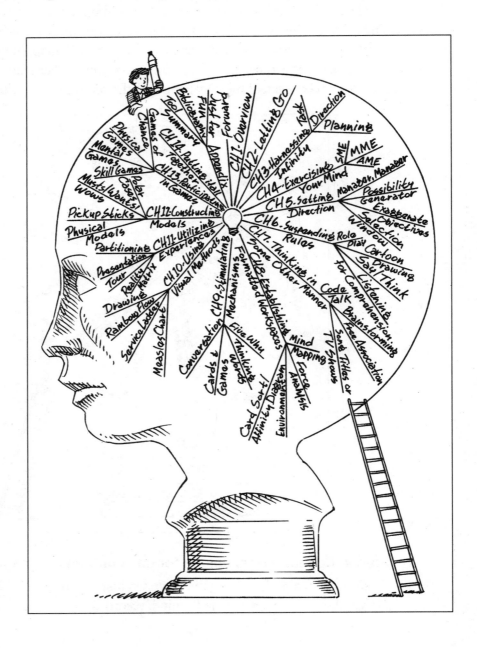

**Step 5. Expand images as long as your creativity continues.**

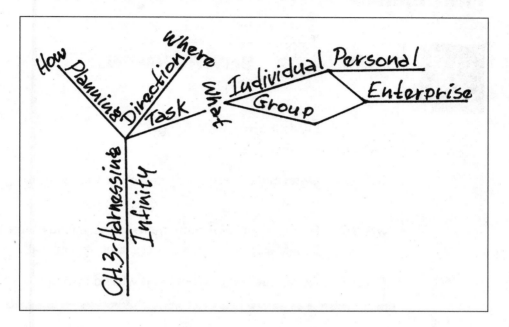

**Step 6. Group together ideas that have common themes by drawing a colored line around all the images in a group, marking them with a code, or redrawing the map to cluster common items together.**

Expand every image on the mind map until your ideas are totally exhausted. As you use mind mapping, you will find that you are increasingly able to draw meaningful images. An example of a completed mind map is shown.

Mind mapping functions best for individuals working on personal issues. It uses provoked creativity. It is best applied to planning. The creative power of this tool is best seen when it is applied to medium time frames. It is a powerful way to unleash the power of the right brain.

*The demands of our creative abilities have doubled in every generation.*
    PETER F. DRUCKER

# Environment

**ENVIRONMENT**

**Type:** "Aha"
**Issue:** Direction, planning, doing
**Who:** Individual

**Step 1.** Determine the type of creativity tool you are going to use.

**Step 2.** Set up your environment to make effective use of this tool and to enhance your creativity in general.

**Step 3.** Remember what works and what doesn't.

One of the most important and overlooked creative tools used in a formatted work space is the environment itself. The environment includes the physical space, the furnishings of the space, the lighting, the music, and other physical features. You encourage "Aha" creativity by changing your environment.

Break out of your comfort zone and make changes to the place where you are working and living. Change your associates, the music that you listen to, and your reading matter. Your paradigm is your approach to situations. To become creative, you must break your paradigm and look at opportunities, problems, and situations from different perspectives. Some ways to change your environment are to take a walk, listen to music, or take a nap. Do the unexpected—for instance, work in a hallway for a day or two. This principle is one reason that so many deals are consummated on the golf course or in the club. The change in environment enables you to see things differently and to be more creative.

A formatted work space can help you to be appropriately creative; its lack will curtail your creativity. Your work space should be a prime consideration as you determine your approach to creativity.

Each of us processes information in a unique fashion. The way we process information relates to different areas of the brain. Some of us are most comfortable fantasizing and imagining that which has not yet occurred. Some people are most comfortable using their feelings; they are comfortable approaching information from the humanistic and sensitive part of the self. Some people's favored thinking style concerns form and structure; they prefer to focus on the way things relate to other things. Still other people prefer to think about facts and data. In this chapter, we talked about creating a formatted work space, a place in life where one can view reality from his or her comfort zone. A formatted work space provides structured ways of achieving creativity, using one's preferred thinking approach.

To maximize creativity, a formatted work space must

- ► Combine different thinking approaches to force us to use more of the whole brain.
- ► Include the physical characteristics of the space in which we work and think.
- ► Use different methodologies to stimulate our creative forces.
- ► Be fun.
- ► Stimulate all of our senses.
- ► Allow both sides of our brains to work together.

Scientists often state that individuals use only a small portion of their thinking capacity. Creating appropriate formatted work spaces can help us all be more creative. A formatted work space might be a garden or a special room within your home or office complex. It may be a methodology such as mind mapping or drawing relationships on a flip chart. It could be something as creative as embarking on a guided fantasy, taking a nap, going for a walk, disengaging from the rest of the world though meditation, or merely closing your eyes and listening to music. Using a formatted work space evokes insights that you might not achieve in another manner.

# Just for Fun

How many triangles are in this figure?

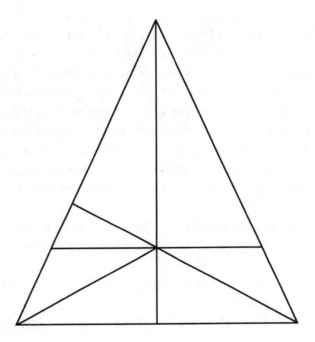

Our preferred answer is in Appendix B.

# 9

# Stimulating Mechanisms: Focusing Your Energy

**H**umans communicate creative ideas by means of words. Words, then, make an excellent catalyst to toggle our minds to call forth new ideas. Although words are plentiful and they are free, most of us do not have very rich vocabularies. Common speech requires only several hundred words. Whereas we typically have vocabularies of thousands of words, there are indeed tens of thousands of words available to us.

In this chapter, we will look at techniques for using this rich reservoir of words to stimulate creative thinking. Words can be used by individuals alone, or they can be used as part of group activities, in group creative processes. Word-based techniques help move our thoughts along and stimulate new ideas, whether the words occur in conversation, appear on cards that are part of a deck, are used individually to stimulate thought, or belong to a set. In each of these four situations and many others, words are used repetitively. A series of steps is often required to get the creative juices flowing. As usual, we encourage you to modify each tool to meet your needs. A word does not evoke the same thought in everyone's mind. Collect your own list of stimulating words, and find the best place for you to use them.

One tool uses evocative questions beginning with "Why." This is the favorite tool of every five-year-old. Youngsters ask Why, Why, Why, Why until with the fourth or fifth question, they get to the root of the matter. Another tool is a checklist of idea-spurring questions. A third tool uses a deck of cards, each one addressing specific issues or stimulating ideas. The fourth tool revolves around communication through conversation.

## Five "Whys"

**CUE CARD**

### FIVE "WHYS"

**Type:** Structured
**Issue:** Doing
**Who:** Group

**Step 1.** Ask "Why" in relation to an opportunity, problem, or situation.

**Step 2.** Ask "Why" in relation to the answer for the first "Why."

**Step 3.** Ask "Why" in relation to the answer for the second "Why."

**Step 4.** Ask "Why" in relation to the answer for the third "Why."

**Step 5.** Ask "Why" in relation to the answer for the fourth "Why."

**Step 6.** Continue this process until you reach a point where a creative idea or solution is possible.

The five "Whys" technique helps you systematically discover vital information. Use it to analyze root causes or develop penetrating questions that require creative solutions.

## Example: Using Five "Whys"

### Step 1. Ask "Why" in relation to an opportunity, problem, or situation.

▶ Why does our product have poor quality, and/or why does the service associated with our product have poor quality?

There are obviously many detailed causes, such as incorrect product definition, incorrect design, incompatibility of design with production, incorrect production, incorrect and/or inappropriate representation during the sales process, incorrect service, incorrect service information, etc.

The generic answer is that the product was not correct, sales were not correct, and/or service related to the product was not correct.

### Step 2. Ask "Why" in relation to the answer for the first "Why."

▶ Why was the product incorrect, and/or why was the associated service incorrect?

For each of the detailed causes, there is a detailed answer: The product definition process was inadequate, the design process was inadequate, the production process was inadequate, and so on.

The generic answer is that the overall process for developing and producing the product and its related systems was inadequate. The answer also points to insufficient knowledge and skills on the part of the people using the processes.

### Step 3. Ask "Why" in relation to the answer for the second "Why."

▶ Why was the total process for developing and producing the product and its related systems inadequate, and why did the people lack the required knowledge and skills?

Again, there are many answers, but they fall into a pattern. There is no clear locus of responsibility for defining and improving the process. The managers do not have the knowledge and skills needed to make the improvements. No resources are allocated for these activities. The improvements are not part of the business plan. The education and training plan does not encompass all the organizational requirements. There is no reward, recognition, or promotion for achievements in these areas within the selection systems.

The generic answer is that the business plan and management of the organization do not recognize the importance of the organizational process, knowledge, and skills.

### Step 4. Ask "Why" in relation to the answer for the third "Why."

▶ Why is the importance of the organization's processes, knowledge, and skills not recognized by the organization's business plan and management?

The senior leadership does not understand. If senior leadership understood, they would act.

### Step 5. Ask "Why" in relation to the answer for the fourth "Why."

▶ Why does senior leadership not understand?

There are many answers relating to current and past paradigms, beliefs, education, culture, societal norms, and so forth.

### Step 6. Continue this process until you reach a point where a creative idea or solution is possible.

▶ Do you need to continue?

The best answer here is "It depends." You may have enough information to spur your creativity before answering any specific "Why," or you may need to ask why several more times.

The five "Whys" method functions best for groups working on enterprise issues. It uses a very structured style of creativity. It is best applied to analysis of tasks. The creative power of this tool is best seen when it is applied to short time frames. This tool is excellent for getting to the root causes of situations.

*A paradox is what you get when you give up thinking.*

# Thinking Words

## THINKING WORDS

**Type:**   Nonlinear
**Issue:**   Doing
**Who:**   Group

**Step 1.**   Isolate the opportunity, problem, or situation you want to think about.

**Step 2.**   Ask CREATES questions about each stage of the opportunity, problem, or situation, and see what ideas emerge.

The thinking words technique provides a checklist of questions or ideas to investigate. It allows you to apply a structure to your creativity. A number of different types of words, representing different structures, are used to spur questions. One type of thinking word is any action verb; another is an acronym. The acronym we use most frequently to unleash creative power is CREATES.

**C** Combine
**R** Rearrange/Reverse
**E** Exaggerate
**A** Adapt
**T** Transform
**E** Eliminate
**S** Substitute

## Example: Using Thinking Words

### Step 1. Isolate the opportunity, problem, or situation you want to think about.

▶ You manufacture traditional wire paper clips, and you want to improve your product.

### Step 2. Ask CREATES questions about each stage of the opportunity, problem, or situation, and see what new ideas emerge.

**Combine**  Much creative thinking involves combinations of ideas. Combining is the process of putting together previously unrelated ideas, goods, or services to create something new. To combine ideas, ask questions such as these:

▶ What ideas can be combined?
▶ Can I combine purposes?
▶ Can the combination be an assortment?
▶ Can the combination be a blend, alloy, or ensemble?
▶ Can units be combined?
▶ What other articles can be merged with this one?
▶ How can I package a combination?
▶ What can I combine to multiply the possible uses?
▶ What materials can I combine?
▶ What appeals can I combine?

**Rearrange/Reverse**  Rearranging what we know in order to find out what we do not know is often a part of creativity. Rearrangement usually offers countless alternatives for ideas, goods, and services. Reversing your perspective on your ideas, goods, or services opens up your thinking. Look at opposites, and you will see things you normally miss. To help you rearrange or reverse, ask yourself questions such as these:

▶ What other arrangement might be better?
▶ Can the components be interchanged?
▶ Is there another possible pattern or layout?

▶ Can I change the order or sequence?

▶ Can I change the pace?

▶ Is the schedule fixed, or can it be changed?

▶ What are the negatives?

▶ Should I turn it around?

▶ What if it were pointing down instead of up?

▶ What if it were backward?

▶ Can roles be reversed?

▶ What do I not expect?

**Exaggerate**  Many individuals believe that bigger is better. People often perceive objects they value highly as being larger than objects they value less.

**Exaggeration in one way or another can trigger your creativity.**

Search for ways to exaggerate, magnify, add to, or multiply your idea, product, or service. To exaggerate, ask questions like these:

- ▶ What can be exaggerated, made larger, magnified, or extended?
- ▶ What can be exaggerated or overstated?
- ▶ What can be added?
- ▶ What can be made stronger, higher, or longer?
- ▶ Can I add extra features?
- ▶ Can I do this more often?
- ▶ Can it take more time?
- ▶ What can add extra value?
- ▶ What can be duplicated?
- ▶ How could I carry this to a dramatic extreme?

*The man who says it cannot be done should not interrupt the man doing it.*
CHINESE PROVERB

**Adapt**  One paradox of creativity is that in order to think originally, one must first be familiar with the ideas of others. Adaptation involves using others' ideas and changing them to satisfy one's needs. To become expert at adaptation, ask questions such as these:

- ▶ What else is like this?
- ▶ What other ideas does this suggest?
- ▶ Does the past offer a parallel?
- ▶ What could I copy?
- ▶ Whom could I emulate?
- ▶ What idea could I incorporate?
- ▶ What other process could be adapted?
- ▶ What different contexts can I put my idea in?
- ▶ What ideas outside my field can I incorporate?
- ▶ What else can this be used for?
- ▶ Are there new ways to use this as it is?
- ▶ What other uses are there if it is modified?
- ▶ What else can be made from this?
- ▶ Are there other markets for this?
- ▶ Can this be extended?

**Transform**  Just about any aspect of anything can be transformed. It is up to you to find those things that can be transformed and make the transformations. To transform your ideas, ask questions like these:

- ▶ How can this be altered for the better?
- ▶ What can be transformed or modified?
- ▶ Is there a new twist that can be added?
- ▶ How can I change meaning, color, motion, sound, odor, form, or shape?
- ▶ What new name can I use?
- ▶ What other changes can I make?
- ▶ What changes can be made in the plans, process, or marketing?
- ▶ What other form could this take?
- ▶ How else can I package this?

**Eliminate**  Creative ideas sometimes come from repeated trimming or elimination of portions. By eliminating portions, you can gradually narrow your idea to the part or function that is really necessary. You may find it is appropriate for another use. Find things to reduce, eliminate, streamline, omit, and miniaturize by asking questions such as these:

- ▶ What if this were smaller?
- ▶ What should I omit?
- ▶ Should I divide it?
- ▶ What if I split it up or separate it into different parts?
- ▶ What happens if I understate it?
- ▶ Can it be streamlined, miniaturized, condensed, or compacted?
- ▶ Can something be subtracted or deleted?
- ▶ Can the rules be eliminated?
- ▶ Can the paradigm be changed?
- ▶ What is not necessary?

**Substitute**  You can substitute things, places, procedures, people, ideas, and even emotions. Substitution is a trial-and-error method of replacing one thing with another until you find the right idea. To find ideas using substitution, ask questions like these:

- ▶ What can be substituted?
- ▶ Who else can do it?
- ▶ What else can be used?

- ▶ Can the rules be changed?
- ▶ Are there other materials that will work?
- ▶ Is another process or procedure better?
- ▶ Can I accomplish this somewhere else?
- ▶ Can I follow a different approach to produce the same or a better result?
- ▶ What else can I use instead of this?
- ▶ What other component part can I use?

In your paper clip design, you might choose to substitute plastic for metal, add colors for marketing attractiveness and for color-coding applications, add a tab for visibility, change the design to make it function better, and transform the packaging to provide a built-in holder.

The thinking words technique functions best for groups working on enterprise issues. It uses nonlinear creativity. It is best applied to analysis of tasks. The creative power of this tool is best seen when it is applied to short time frames. This tool is excellent for analyzing situations and creating alternatives to something that already exists.

## Cards and Games

**CARDS AND GAMES**

**Type:** Nonlinear
**Issue:** Doing
**Who:** Group

**Step 1.** Determine in what area creative breakthrough is required.

**Step 2.** Acquire the appropriate card set or game.

**Step 3.** Assemble the right group if required.

**Step 4.** Use the card deck or game as a mechanism to change the paradigm under which you function.

Many types of cards and games can be used to stimulate creativity. Cards and games provide an enjoyable way for people to break down some of their normal barriers. They can help you to gain insights into areas you may not have considered. There are commercially prepared games and decks of cards that focus on numerous areas such as technology, personal interaction, future trends, and values determination. If you cannot find one to address your situation, do not be afraid to develop your own.

## Example: Using Cards and Games

### Step 1. Determine in what area creative breakthrough is required.

▶ You own a restaurant and want to use the latest technology to improve the accuracy with which orders are handled.

### Step 2. Acquire the appropriate card set or game.

▶ You buy a Technotrends™ Card Pack by Daniel Burrus.

### Step 3. Assemble the right group if required.

▶ You, two of your chefs, two of your servers, and two good customers get together for two hours to use the deck of cards.

### Step 4. Use the card deck or game as a mechanism to change the paradigm under which you function.

▶ The creative result of your group's meeting is that every table will have a Personal Digital Assistant (PDA) displaying all the menu choices. The customer or server places the order at the table, using the PDA. The order is transmitted to a large computer screen visible to the chefs. When the order is ready, the server is paged on a soundless beeper and can immediately deliver the customer's food. The PDA at the table also pages the server's soundless beeper if the customer needs anything else. The bill is printed at the table. If the customer pays by credit or debit card, the transaction is completed on the PDA at the table, and the receipt is printed at the table.

Cards and games function best for groups working on enterprise issues. They use provoked creativity. This approach is best applied to planning. The creative power of this tool is best seen when it is applied to medium and long time frames. This tool is excellent for examining new and emerging technologies.

## Conversation

**CONVERSATION**

**Type:** "Aha"
**Issue:** Planning
**Who:** Individual

**Step 1.** Engage in conversation with others, preferably those who do not share your viewpoint and background.

**Step 2.** Listen to what is said.

**Step 3.** Apply what is said to your own situation.

Conversation is one of the most overlooked and misunderstood creativity resources. Because conversation is often informal, many people engaging in it do not feel that they are being creative. Informal conversation often results in "Aha" ideas because we allow our preconceived notions to be broken.

This approach to creativity works best in informal settings where a wide range of individuals are involved. Conversation does not need to be structured, but it does need to be practiced. While you are involved in conversations with others, it is important to let your mind roam freely while you talk about specifics. You may wish to play the devil's advocate or to adopt a position with which you feel very comfortable. The important thing is to listen to what others are saying and apply what they say to your own ideas.

Conversation as an approach to creativity functions best for individuals working on personal issues. It evokes "Aha" creativity. It is best applied to planning. The creative power of conversation is best seen when it is applied to medium time frames.

Humans usually use words to be creative. We think in words, we speak in words, we communicate in words. Words make an excellent catalyst to toggle our minds and generate new ideas. Mechanisms based on words include

▶ Acronyms,
▶ Cards,
▶ Physical objects, and
▶ Games.

These mechanisms use words to trigger our creativity. Words that have proven in the past to be good generators of ideas are such simple questions as

▶ Why?
▶ How? and
▶ What if?

Systematically using words stimulates ideas and generates movement along your creative path. The use of your own favorite words causes you to move into your creative space and allows you to look at things in new and innovative ways. We encourage you to be creative in your use of all tools and techniques presented throughout this book.

## Just for Fun

 How many boxes do you see?

Appendix B contains a solution or two if you care to peek.

# 10

# Using Visual Methods: Taking a Different View

**G**rowing up with television has heightened the visual sense of those born after World War II. One can also argue that humans have been visually oriented since the first cave dwellers drew pictures of game on the cave walls to communicate to their descendants what they had seen and experienced. A few low-tech approaches to creating a visual image, a new idea, a new concept, or a new breakthrough use flip charts, adhesive notes, and marking pens. Like all of the methods presented in this book, graphic and visual representations can work for individuals or teams of people. An exciting dimension of visual representations is often overlooked. A walk down the aisle of any office supply store or art store reveals a rich array of fluid markers, felt-tipped pens and colored papers; most of these items are available for under $10. These simple supplies can provide a rich resource for creating new and dynamic relationships.

The four tools we have chosen to present in this chapter are rainbow flow charting, drawing, the measles chart, and the service ladder. Although many people are afraid to put pen or pencil to paper and are inhibited by their perceived lack of artistic skill, visual methods do not depend for their effectiveness upon one's artistic talent. In this chapter we mean visualization not in the pure artistic sense but in the conceptual, graphic sense. Thus the tools we have chosen do not require a Master of Fine Arts degree or even a fine hand. They require only a desire to create and communicate new and exciting relationships in a visual manner.

These visual renderings are meant to travel. They should be hung up on walls to stimulate discussion and debate. They should show coffee stains as others contribute their ideas and generate new and exciting relationships. Again, some of us need a license to draw, a license to visualize. The four tools described in this chapter provide just such a license, allowing each of us, whatever our level of artistic ability, to jump in and have some fun. Everyone liked to draw in first grade; there is no reason why we still cannot continue to draw and present relationships to create new and exciting insights.

## Rainbow Flow Charting

### RAINBOW FLOW CHARTING

**Type:** Structured
**Issue:** Doing
**Who:** Group

**Step 1.** Determine the process or product you want to study.

**Step 2.** Draw a diagram of the product or process, using symbols and colors.

**Step 3.** Describe how the process works or should work by placing descriptions in the symbols.

**Step 4.** Analyze the differences between what is and what should be.

One of the first steps in studying a process is to make a flow chart. This means writing down, step by step, what happens during the process. This is necessary because it will give you a foundation for your process improvement study.

To develop a flow chart, you may want to observe work as it progresses through your unit and record each step as it happens. You may also want to talk to employees who are involved in the process. At the start of a process improvement study, it may be useful to develop two flow charts—one showing how the process should be running according to documented procedures, the other based on the process you actually observe. Comparing these two different flow charts for the same process will give you insight into sources of rework or complexity in the process.

In developing a flow chart, you should use distinct symbols for process steps, decisions, connections, start and end, and process flow. Different colors should be used to identify different individuals or departments involved in different activities. You can add additional information, such as measurements and checkpoints.

*If we were able to force our brain to work at only half its capacity, we could without difficulty whatever, learn 40 languages, memorize the large Soviet encyclopedia from cover to cover, and complete the required courses of dozens of colleges.*

DR. W. ROSS ADEY AND ASSOCIATES

## Example: Using Rainbow Flow Charting

**Step 1. Determine the process or product to be studied.**

▶ Hourly employee pay

**Step 2. Draw a diagram of the product or process, using symbols and colors.**

## Step 3. Describe how the process works or should work by placing descriptions in the symbols.

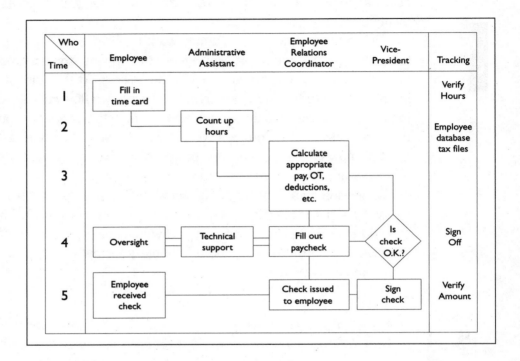

| Who / Time | Employee | Administrative Assistant | Employee Relations Coordinator | Vice-President | Tracking |
|---|---|---|---|---|---|
| 1 | Fill in time card | | | | Verify Hours |
| 2 | | Count up hours | | | Employee database tax files |
| 3 | | | Calculate appropriate pay, OT, deductions, etc. | | |
| 4 | Oversight | Technical support | Fill out paycheck | Is check O.K.? | Sign Off |
| 5 | Employee received check | | Check issued to employee | Sign check | Verify Amount |

## Step 4. Analyze the differences between what is and what should be.

▶ In the case shown in our diagram, the "actual" and the "should be" were identical. However, because the process was analyzed, the vice-president's sign-off was eliminated because the employee relations co-ordinator had budgetary responsibility for the process.

Rainbow flow charting functions best for groups working on enterprise issues. It uses very structured creativity. It can easily be applied to tasks. The creative power of this tool is best seen when it is applied to short time frames. It provides a highly visual way to examine who is responsible for each step in a process.

# Drawing

**CUE CARD**

## DRAWING

**Type:**  Nonlinear
**Issue:**  Direction, planning, doing
**Who:**  Individual

**Step 1.**  Determine the process or product you want to study.

**Step 2.**  Draw your issue as something else or from a different perspective.

**Step 3.**  Explain your drawing.

Drawing helps you examine the boundaries, rules, and regulations you unconsciously apply to yourself and your situation. Your rules, regulations, boundaries, and beliefs cause you to distort information to make it fit into your world; they constitute a filter for your world that may in fact be a hindrance to your creativity.

Using a drawing to depict your world opens new avenues of looking at what you do. The less realistic the drawing, the more likely it will cause you to challenge a rule or belief that has prevented you from making creative breakthroughs.

## Example: Using Drawing

### Step 1. Determine the process or product to be studied.

▶ Customers do not seem to trust our used car salespeople.

**Step 2. Draw your issue as something else or from a different perspective.**

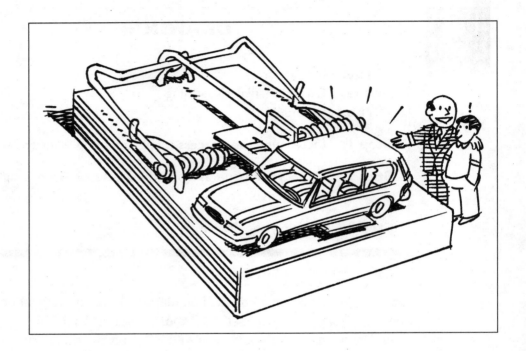

**Step 3. Explain your drawing.**

▶ From the customer's perspective, our car deals look like bait in a trap. We need to change our basic sales approach to focus more on the needs of the customer.

Drawing is a method that functions best for individuals working on enterprise issues. It uses nonlinear creativity. It can be effectively applied to direction setting and planning. The creative power of this tool is best seen when it is applied to medium time frames. It provides a highly visual way to challenge barriers, beliefs, rules, and regulations.

# Measles Chart

**MEASLES CHART**

**Type:** Provoked
**Issue:** Doing
**Who:** Group

**Step 1.** Determine the process or product you want to study.

**Step 2.** Draw a diagram of the process or product.

**Step 3.** Mark errors on the diagram where they occur.

**Step 4.** Analyze the results.

The measles chart is a type of check sheet on which both the frequency and the location of errors are recorded. Sometimes a breakthrough will occur when you know the location of errors as well as their frequency. The diagram need not be highly detailed. You might use a different symbol or color for each type of error. Display the measles chart where everyone can see it easily. Creative power is unleashed when the analysis begins. Suspend your normal rules and beliefs, and ask questions from a different point of view.

## Example: Using a Measles Chart

### Step 1. Determine the process or product to be studied.

The problem, which occurred during World War II, was that not all Allied bombers returned from their raids on the European continent.

▶ The product to be studied was the Allied bombers.

**Step 2. Draw a diagram of the product or process.**

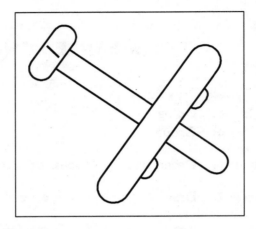

**Step 3. Mark errors on the diagram where they occur.**

▶ Every bullet hole was marked on every plane that returned.

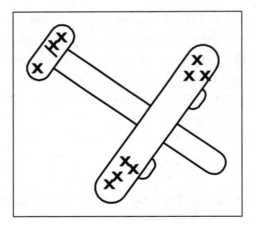

**Step 4. Analyze the results.**

▶ After the bullet holes on all of the planes were analyzed, the decision was made to add more armor to the planes. The armor was not added where the holes had occurred; rather it was added where they had not occurred. The creative reasoning behind this decision was as follows: Because the planes that returned all had holes in the wings and tail, those that did not return probably had holes in the fuselage and cockpit. If creative thought had not been applied, extra armor would have been added to the wing and tail surfaces.

The measles chart functions best for groups working on enterprise issues. It uses provoked creativity. It can easily be applied to tasks. The creative power of this tool is best seen when it is applied to short time frames. This tool provides a highly visual way to examine problems.

# Service Ladder

**SERVICE LADDER**

**Type:** "Aha"
**Issue:** Doing
**Who:** Group

**Step 1.** Define the process you want to examine.

**Step 2.** Map the waiting and working times.

**Step 3.** Analyze where you can eliminate waiting time.

The service ladder technique gives you a way to eliminate superfluous waiting time from your processes and to design new processes without adding unnecessary waiting time. The goal is to design a wall instead of a ladder; this concept would represent a perfect process with no waiting time. It is rarely possible to achieve a perfect process, but you should aim for a process that is efficient in your environment.

# Example: Using the Service Ladder

## Step 1. Define the process you want to examine.

▶ Obtaining a building permit

## Step 2. Map the waiting and working times.

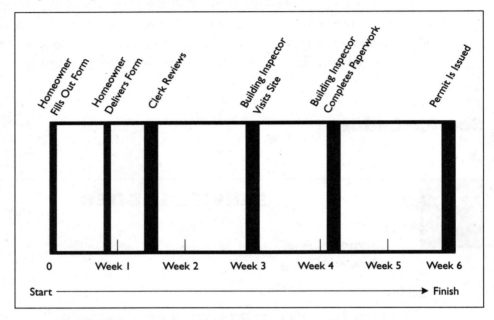

## Step 3. Analyze where waiting time can be eliminated.

▶ The homeowner could have filled out the form at the town hall and eliminated one of the white spaces. Many other opportunities could also be investigated.

The service ladder functions best for groups working on issues that face enterprises. It calls on "Aha" creativity. It is best applied to tasks. The creative power of this tool is best seen when it is applied to time frames of months and even years. It provides a way for groups to examine what they do within organizations and to open new lines of communication.

This chapter presented a set of tools that provide visual ways to improve creative efforts, to get things to be the way we want them to be.

Developing new and innovative approaches to producing results can lead to methods, processes, and outputs that are associated with fewer errors, defects, mistakes, and instances of unhappiness. Some visual aids for looking at situations are measles charts and diagrams using color, arrows, and shading to indicate the desirable and undesirable parts of the process or situation.

Creative insights can be used to generate new and better ways of achieving desired results. Processes can also be modified physically to guarantee the desired results. It is impossible to put your hand into a running clothes dryer because opening the door turns the machine off. You cannot leave the light on in your refrigerator because closing the door turns the light off. Processes—physical realities—can be modified and re-created to guarantee desired outcomes. Some cars will not start unless the seat belts are engaged. Creating new and better physical realities generates error-proof results.

## Just for Fun

 How many boxes do you see?

Appendix B contains one answer and another question!

# 11

# Utilizing Experiences: Fostering Your Capabilities

Creativity is not a spectator sport. You cannot learn to be creative by watching others be creative; you cannot create by watching others create; you cannot create in a neutral and passive way. Creating new ideas, creating that which did not exist before, requires involvement. You must jump in and be part of the creative process.

As we have already noted, the status quo is the result of pressures and forces that define the way one is. To break the status quo and move on to something new, quite often you must physically move, get out of your work space. Take a tour; go see something different; visit another organization or another person. See, feel, taste, and touch some new ideas in action that will stimulate you to bigger and better things. Ideas alone will not change the world. Change requires ideas plus action. Hollow rhetoric is just that—a lot of words that do not amount to much.

One way to transform theory into practice and ideas into action is to partition or divide the situation into its underlying assumptions. Another is to post a simple three-column list called a reality matrix, listing what must be done, who will do it, and when it will be done. The purpose is to associate ideas with appropriate actions. Information and ideas stored away in computers or locked in large reports are not in a user-friendly form. The presentation of ideas can create a dynamic synergism of its own; it can give rise to a new and wonderful set of ideas. Getting out and visiting, seeing a new place, taking a tour, and always having a reality matrix on hand presenting end results are methods presented in this chapter. A very specific way of getting to a new place, a new idea, is to partition what we currently have into parts, into pieces. A series of repetitive steps will take us into a new space.

## Partitioning

**CUE CARD**

### PARTITIONING

**Type:** Structured
**Issue:** Doing
**Who:** Group

**Step 1.** Define the opportunity, problem, or situation.

**Step 2.** Divide the problem into the elements that make up your cultural frame of reference.

**Step 3.** Divide these elements into underlying assumptions.

**Step 4.** Develop a solution to overcome the assumptions.

Partitioning is a powerful vehicle for moving from abstract thoughts to methods that can be implemented. There is often a gap between theory and practice. When you start with the basic frame of reference and the assumptions that constitute it, you have the basis for creative solutions to problems you do not know exist. Partitioning is the basis for many reengineering and reverse engineering projects.

# Example: Using Partitioning

## Step 1. Define the problem, opportunity, or situation.

▶ Our company is not taking advantage of our vendors' payment terms of 2 percent if paid within 10 days. Instead, we pay within 30 days and pay net price.

```
┌─────────────────┐
│    No 2%        │
│   Discount      │
└─────────────────┘
```

## Step 2. Divide the problem into the elements that make up your cultural frame of reference.

▶ In our company, payments are not made until all incoming materials have been inspected, the bill of lading (BOL) has been signed and sent

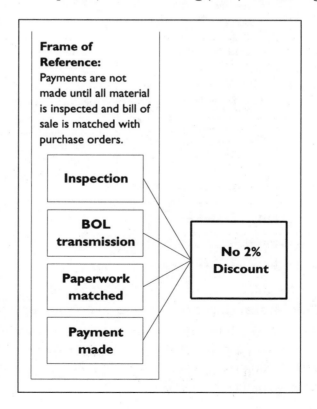

to purchasing, and the BOL has been matched with the original purchase order to ensure that the product received is the one that was ordered.

### Step 3. Divide these elements into underlying assumptions.

▶ One of our underlying assumptions is that all work as well as all incoming parts must be inspected to ensure that we produce quality products.

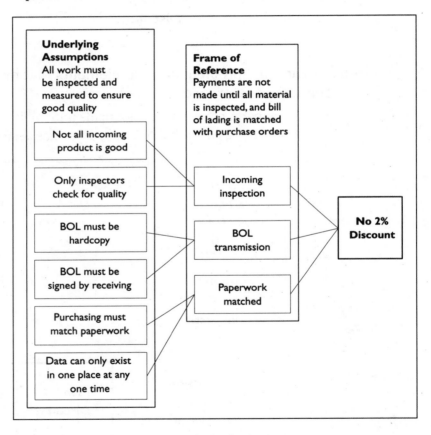

### Step 4. Develop a solution to overcome assumptions.

▶ One solution that overcomes many of the assumptions is to install on the receiving dock a computer terminal where the incoming BOL could be matched on line with the purchase order. Responsibility for the quality of incoming parts should be shifted to the supplier; this would eliminate the need for incoming inspection. This solution enables the company to maximize the discount for early payment.

The partitioning method functions best for groups working on enterprise issues. It uses very structured creativity. It is best applied to analysis of tasks. The creative power of this tool is best seen when it is applied to short time frames. This tool is excellent for getting to basic assumptions and beliefs.

*We don't need more strength or more ability or greater opportunity. What we need is to use what we have.*
BASIL S. WALSH

## Reality Matrix

### REALITY MATRIX

**Type:** Nonlinear
**Issue:** Doing
**Who:** Group

**Step 1.** Define the steps in the process.

**Step 2.** Identify who is responsible for each step.

**Step 3.** Define when each step will be done.

**Step 4.** Analyze for missing steps and completion times.

The reality matrix gives you a way to check on a process or idea to ensure that it is completely thought through. The matrix provides a list of what, by whom, and when things must be done. This list enables you to unleash your creativity in areas that are not addressed in your current process or plan.

# Example: Using a Reality Matrix

## Step 1. Define the steps in the process.

▶ The process is obtaining a building permit.

| What | | |
|---|---|---|
| Fill out form | | |
| Deliver form | | |
| Review form | | |
| Visit site | | |
| Complete paperwork | | |
| Issue permit | | |

## Step 2. Identify who is responsible for each step.

| What | Who | |
|---|---|---|
| Fill out form | Homeowner | |
| Deliver form | Homeowner's husband | |
| Review form | Town clerk | |
| Visit site | Building inspector | |
| Complete paperwork | Building inspector | |
| Issue permit | Planning manager | |

## Step 3. Define when each step will be done.

| What | Who | When |
|---|---|---|
| Fill out form | Homeowner | Week 1 Monday |
| Deliver form | Homeowner's husband | Week 1 Friday |
| Review form | Town clerk | Week 2 Thursday |
| Visit site | Building inspector | Week 3 Wednesday |
| Complete paperwork | Building inspector | Week 4 Tuesday |
| Issue permit | Planning manager | Week 5 Friday |

### Step 4. Analyze for missing steps and completion times.

► By looking at this simple reality matrix, the homeowner is able to see that the architect's review is missing.

The reality matrix functions best for groups working on enterprise issues. It uses nonlinear creativity. It is best applied to analysis of tasks. The creative power of this tool is best seen when it is applied to short time frames. This tool is excellent for detecting gaps in plans or processes.

# Presentation

**CUE CARD**

---

# PRESENTATION

**Type:** Provoked
**Issue:** Planning
**Who:** Group

**Step 1.** Develop your presentation.

**Step 2.** Practice.

**Step 3.** Introduce your subject. Present your work. Conclude with a summary. Allow opportunity for questions. Ask for assistance if required.

---

Your success depends on your involving others. To gain their support, you need to share what you have done and how you have arrived at your creative solution. For best results, follow this simple presentation guideline: Tell them what you are going to tell them, tell them, and then tell them that you told them.

Because a presentation is usually informal, it can benefit from a creative, nontraditional approach. Be sure to practice your presentation until you understand and feel comfortable with the content. Be willing to use song, dance, gestures, computers, and any other media that will give your presentation dynamic impact. Remember that any time you interact with someone else, you are in effect making a presentation.

## Example: Using Presentation

### Step 1. Develop your presentation.

▶ Do not limit yourself to overheads, flip charts, or handouts. Think of unique ways to provide the information you need to convey.

### Step 2. Practice.

▶ Even if you know what you are going to present, practice several times. If possible, find a practice audience such as your significant other, friends, or relatives. Use a mirror if no one is available.

### Step 3. Introduce your subject. Present your work. Conclude with a summary. Allow opportunity for questions. Ask for assistance if required.

▶ Use the three-tell method. Tell your listeners, quickly and briefly, what you are going to tell them. Tell them in detail what you want them to know; try to convey information, not just data. Finally, tell them what you told them: Complete the presentation with a concise summary of the important points. Give the audience time to formulate and ask questions. Ask for a decision or closure if it is appropriate.

A good presentation is best for groups working on enterprise issues. It uses provoked creativity. It is best applied to planning issues. The creative power of this tool is best seen when it is applied to medium time frames. This tool is excellent for conveying information to many people at once and for building support for creative ideas.

*A mind stretched to a new idea never goes back to its original dimension.*
    OLIVER WENDELL HOLMES

# Tour

> # TOUR
>
> **Type:** "Aha"
> **Issue:** Direction
> **Who:** Individual
>
> **Step 1.** Determine type of tour.
>
> **Step 2.** Go. Observe.
>
> **Step 3.** Apply learnings to your environment.

There are a number of different types of tours that you can take. Choose the type that best meets your objective. If you have nothing in mind, a tour will probably bring nothing to mind. In the latter case, a tour can be a great waste of resources. However, when you keep your mind open and look for new ideas, it can be a tremendous value.

## Example: Taking a Tour

Following are some suggestions for tours. Many others are possible.

- ▶ The simplest tour is of your own environment. Try to observe your surroundings as if you were seeing them for the first time.
- ▶ A second type of tour is a visit to a supplier. Observe what they do and how they do it.
- ▶ A third type of tour features visits to competitors. Look for what they do well and what they do not do well.
- ▶ A fourth type of tour gets you out of your comfortable surroundings and moves you into surroundings that are unfamiliar.

▶ The most exciting tours—of whatever type—are those that open your mind to new experiences and learning. Changing your surroundings enables you to open your mind to new, creative environments.

Taking a tour is best for individuals working on enterprise issues. It calls on "Aha" creativity. It is best applied to direction issues. The creative power of this tool is best seen when it is applied to medium and long time frames. This tool is excellent for finding surprise information and germinating creative ideas.

*The new hero is no longer a blue collar worker, a financier, or a manager, but the innovator who combines imaginative knowledge into action. In addition to the health of the organization, the health, development, and self-actualization of people are promoted immeasurably by the creative and innovative process.*
ALVIN TOFFLER

In this chapter we have discussed ways to use experiences to develop creative insights. There are many other methods you can use. Employing a visual representation of the situation, the problem, or the issue for the creative space gives us a chance to think creatively and develop new insights.

The classic picture was developed in the 1920s by Walt Disney, who used storyboarding for his cartoons. That circumstance leads us to conclude that any visual representation can provide a formatted work space for thinking anew about a situation. In today's world we have a great variety of resources for pictorial representation, including

▶ Video recorders,
▶ Instant cameras,
▶ Drawing paper, and
▶ Scissors to cut out a graphic representation of a situation.

All of these methods allow us to create new insights by approaching a situation visually.

Quite often, the problem consists of a series of forces affecting and defining a given situation. We can represent the dynamics pictorially using tools such as a force field analysis, a cause-and-effect diagram, or a radar chart. A pictorial representation need not be limited to a rendering of something. We can picture something by walking into the world that we need to understand and taking a physical tour. We can walk through the plant or the factory, visit our competitors, visit our vendors, or visit our customers to gain new insights by actually seeing what the relationships are. A picture is truly worth a thousand words, and a visit or tour is worth a thousand pictures.

**Force field analysis** is a simple but very effective way of visually presenting a situation or problem. An estimate is made about how good or bad a situation is. Then the restraining forces and driving forces are defined and pictured on the analysis sheet as arrows pointing in the appropriate directions.

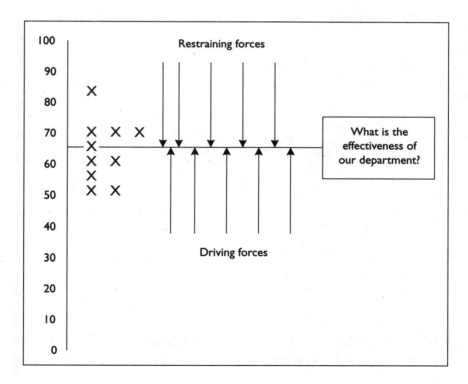

**Cause-and-effect diagrams** are sometimes known as fish-bone diagrams because of their shape. A cause-and-effect diagram is generally used to identify problem solutions. It portrays the relationship between a problem and its possible causes and provides an opportunity for the group to develop, explore, and analyze this relationship graphically.

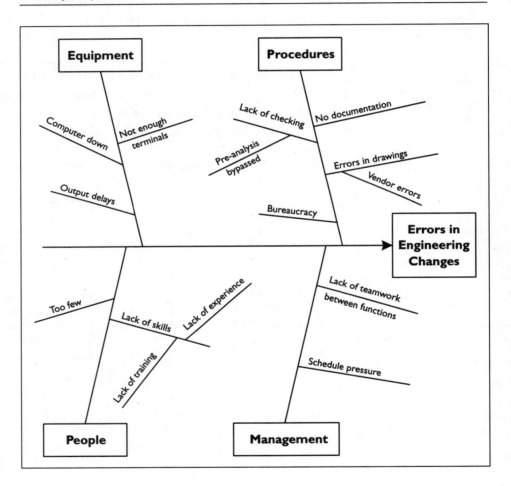

**A radar chart** or a Daetz Diagraph, after Dr. Daetz, who first documented this technique in his doctoral thesis, is used to compare two or more items that have a number (4 to 12) of different parameters that are being compared. It is also called a spider chart.

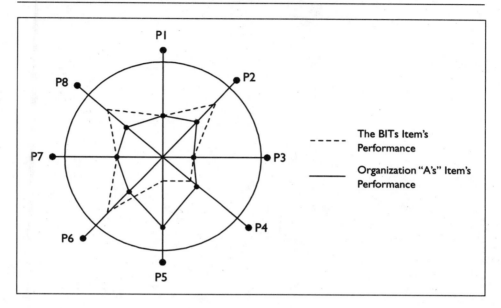

- - - - - The BITs Item's Performance

——— Organization "A's" Item's Performance

# Just for Fun

Are the lines of the square and the triangle straight or curved?

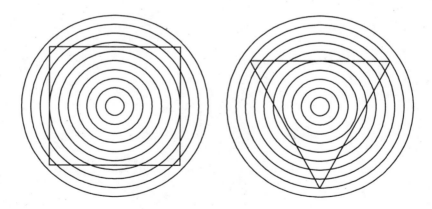

Appendix B contains the answers.

# 12

# Constructing Models: Thinking in Many Dimensions

Letting the mind expand to its fullest and richest potential quite often requires thinking in three or four dimensions. To do this, we may construct mental or physical models that allow us to move beyond words. These models represent either the world as we know it or a new and better world.

A model depicts a creative set of relationships that we are trying to define. In this chapter, we will visit four methods for modeling. The first method provides a way to differentiate among "musts, wants, and wows." The second method allows you to look at polar cases: By examining the extremes of a situation, you are often able to better understand your current position. The third method involves physical models representing the way things interact. The fourth method builds on pick-up sticks: Using these seemingly trivial playthings to represent relationships provides a very powerful method of examining relationships. Modeling along the lines of the extremes also helps one think out of the box, out of the regular, out of the norm, out of one's conditioned responses to most issues. The world would be a simple place if there were only a single issue defining the status quo or the situation that exists.

The way things are results from the interaction of many issues that touch each other at many different points. Developing models as part of a set of tools helps us identify what we must do, what we want to do, and what will excite us if we do it.

## Musts/Wants/Wows

| | |
|---|---|
| **CUE CARD** | **MUST/WANTS/WOWS** |

**MUST/WANTS/WOWS**

**Type:** Structured
**Issue:** Doing
**Who:** Group

**Step 1.** Define your target.

**Step 2.** Create a matrix.

**Step 3.** Generate a list of needs, sort the list into levels, and load the needs into the matrix.

Musts/wants/wows is a technique for identifying what you must do to satisfy whomever you are going to try to satisfy. It provides a method for categorizing different levels of needs. Knowing what you must do enables you to get by. Knowing what is wanted enables you to be successful. Knowing what is exciting enables you to excel.

### Example: Using Musts/Wants/Wows

**Step 1: Define whom you are targeting with your creative ideas. There are three types or levels of need.**

► Musts are items that are simply taken for granted or assumed. For instance, you assume the food in a restaurant will not make you sick, but you do not mention that when you give the server your order. Musts alone will not provide satisfaction, but they can prevent dissatisfaction.

► Wants are requirements or specifications that can be described. Wants are generally based on conscious choice. For instance, you choose what food to order and describe how it is to be cooked. Wants can provide satisfaction if the musts have been met. Wants and musts together meet your expectations, but they fail to give you a compelling reason to speak well of the business or to return in the future.

▶ Wows are the extras beyond the expectations. You can't describe a wow because if you could, it would simply be another want or must. For instance, the owner of the restaurant stops by your table to greet you personally. Surprises like this cause you to tell others about products and services that you like. They are the extras that bring customers back again and again. But beware—the wows that are so special will simply become wants over time because you come to expect them.

**Step 2. Create a matrix as shown. Display the need levels across the top and the names of those you must satisfy along the left. Group together those who receive similar products or services.**

| Musts | Wants | Wows |
|-------|-------|------|
|       |       |      |

**Step 3. Generate a list of needs, sort the list of needs into levels, and load the needs into the matrix. The figure shows the matrix filled out for the needs of a business traveler staying at a hotel.**

| Musts | Wants | Wows |
|-------|-------|------|
| Clean sheets | Nonsmoking room | Coffeepot |
| Bed | King-sized bed | Fruit bowl |
| Shampoo | Remote-control TV | Free beverages |
|  | HBO/CNN |  |
|  | Desk |  |
|  | Hair dryer |  |

The musts/wants/wows method functions best for groups working on enterprise issues. It uses very structured creativity. It is best applied to analysis of tasks. The creative power of this tool is best seen when it is applied to short time frames. This tool is excellent for getting to the basic needs of customers, supervisors, and peers.

*All models are wrong, but some models are useful.*
GEORGE BOX

# Polar Cases

**CUE CARD**

# POLAR CASES

**Type:**  Nonlinear
**Issue:**  Direction, planning
**Who:**  Individual

**Step 1.**  Define the situation.

**Step 2.**  Define the best and worst cases for the situation.

**Step 3.**  Determine what you must do to achieve the best case and avoid the worst case.

Polar cases are best thought of as pairs of opposites. They help us achieve better insight into the reasons why things are as they are. Not only does each situation have its polar case, each of these issues is one of many issues that define reality. We look for a culprit. We look for a single answer. Every issue has at least two polar cases or extremes that define its limits. We must free our minds to be creative; we must allow for the possibilities of those two polar cases and think of their relative merits. For any given situation, look at its polar cases.

## Example: Using Polar Cases

### Step 1. Define the situation.

▶ You have been in an accident and are severely injured.

### Step 2. Define the best and worst cases for the situation.

▶ You will regain your physical abilities, or you will be unable to move without assistance.

### Step 3. Determine what you must do to achieve the best case and avoid the worst case.

▶ You undergo surgery and physical therapy to regain your physical abilities. In addition, you learn about homeopathic medicine and learn to control your diet. You actually improve your capabilities.

The polar cases approach functions best for individuals working on personal issues. It uses nonlinear creativity. It is best applied to planning and direction setting. The creative power of this tool is best seen when it is applied to medium and long time frames. This technique is excellent for examining the boundaries of your beliefs.

# Physical Models

**CUE CARD**

## PHYSICAL MODELS

**Type:**  Nonlinear
**Issue:**  Doing
**Who:**  Group

**Step 1.**  Define the situation.

**Step 2.**  Develop a model of the situation, using physical pieces and parts.

At the most fundamental level, it is helpful to build a physical model of a situation. Models can range from exact replicas to broad representations. An exact replica is usually prepared by a professional. Because the objective of making a physical model is to generate creativity, making an exact model is generally not the best approach.

Your model can be made of any material that is available. Some inexpensive materials that lend themselves to this technique include children's building blocks, erector sets, and Tinkertoys.

A physical model allows you to represent forces by sizes and shapes of the pieces used. In our experience, the more detailed and realistic the model is, the less creative energy it generates. When you design your physical model in more abstract terms, you can focus your creative energies on developing new relationships.

The physical models approach functions best for groups working on enterprise issues. It uses provoked creativity. It is best applied to planning and tasks. The creative power of this tool is best seen when it is applied to medium and short time frames. This technique is excellent for examining the physical boundaries you confront on a daily basis.

# Pick-up Sticks

## PICK-UP STICKS

**Type:** "Aha"
**Issue:** Direction
**Who:** Individual

**Step 1.** Define each stick as a force that has impact on you.

**Step 2.** Define your position in relation to the force.

**Step 3.** Examine the interactions between this force and others that have impact on you.

The childhood game of pick-up sticks becomes a very effective way of modeling forces that define our world. The scattered sticks illustrate the configuration of forces that define any situation. You can think of each stick as an issue or force that represents the pressures in the real world that define the way things are. The ends of each stick are the opposite positions relative to a given issue (e.g., if the issue is how to staff an organization, the two ends are hiring part-time or temporary employees versus hiring full-time employees). The appropriate position to take depends on the interaction of all the pick-up sticks that represent our organization. We need to see where the "staffing" stick intersects with the sticks representing other issues. Pick-up sticks provide a mental model of reality for each issue; every stick can be thought of as a driving force. The way each of the pick-up sticks interacts with the others defines our current reality. An individual or an organization typically has 7 to 12 of these key issues. Moving the pick-up sticks and reconfiguring them creates a new way of being, a new interaction among the forces that define you or your organization.

The pick-up sticks approach is best for individuals working on personal issues. It calls on "Aha" creativity. It is best applied to design. The creative power of this tool is best seen when it is applied to long time frames. This technique is excellent for examining the interactions among the forces that have impact on you.

We can never hope to build an exact model of the real world. Our goal in this chapter has been to present some helpful tools and techniques for building models that are reflective and indicative of the real world.

Using a model

► Stimulates new insights.
► Helps you see in more than one dimension.
► Unleashes creative thinking.
► Fosters understanding of the present.
► Allows you to visualize the "what if."

A model is an indication of the way things are. You can also develop a model of the way things should be. When you make such a model, open your mental time event horizon, and allow your model to incorporate the changes that you think the future will bring.

# Just for Fun

Create five crossed pairs.

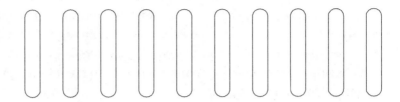

- ▶ A stick moves by jumping over two sticks and lying atop the third.
- ▶ A pair of crossed sticks counts as two sticks.
- ▶ Each move must be in a single direction, but it may be in either direction.
- ▶ Sticks once crossed may not be uncrossed.

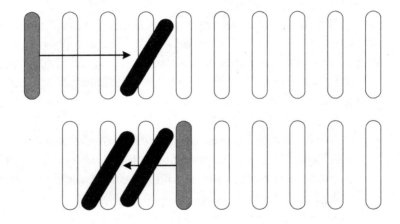

Final configuration:

The solution is in Appendix B.

# 13

# Participating in Games: Facing Uncertainty

The future is by definition uncertain. The past is but prologue to a changing world that may assume any one of infinite numbers of forms and structures. The challenge, then, is to live successfully, to prosper and survive in the face of uncertainty. Uncertainty is a feature of many popular games for children and adults.

Every roll of the dice, every visit to a casino is an experience of the game of life. The probabilities are known, but the outcome is not. We can sharpen our skills for coping with uncertainty by using games that tap the ability to respond instantaneously to a changing set of circumstances. These games can be skill games, physical games, games of chance, or mental games.

As managers of our fate, we must respond appropriately in the face of uncertainty. To practice the necessary skills, we need a practice field, a formatted work space. Games of chance provide opportunities to practice responding under time constraints with creative responses that perhaps did not exist before.

Games are just plain fun. Never overlook the enjoyable element of creativity. The fact that creativity can be hard work does not mean that it cannot be fun at the same time. If you are not having fun, you are doing something wrong!

## Skill Games

### SKILL GAMES

**Type:** Structured
**Issue:** Doing
**Who:** Individual

**Step 1.** Define your opportunity.

**Step 2.** Pick a skill game.

**Step 3.** Use the skill game to help you generate ways to approach your opportunity.

Skill games promote individual creativity. Such games, often created by others, enable us to develop our creativity patterns. Skill games include crossword puzzles, word search puzzles, and jigsaw puzzles. New jigsaw puzzles have three-dimensional aspects that challenge players to stretch their creative abilities even further. One drawback to these prepared games is that there usually is only one preferred answer. Those who are most creative will always search for more than one solution to a given opportunity.

### Example: Using Skill Games

**Step 1. Define your opportunity.**

▶ It takes you over one hour to drive to work.

**Step 2. Pick a skill game.**

▶ Crossword puzzle.

**Step 3. Use the skill game to help you generate possibilities to approach your opportunity.**

The skill game approach functions best for individuals working on personal issues. It uses very structured creativity. It is best applied to tasks. The creative power of this tool is best seen when it is applied to short time frames. It provides a way to examine your issues in relation to something else.

## Physical Games

### PHYSICAL GAMES

**Type:**   Nonlinear
**Issue:**   Doing
**Who:**   Group

**Step 1.**   Define your opportunity.

**Step 2.**   Pick a physical game.

**Step 3.**   Use the physical game to help you generate ways to approach your opportunity.

Physical games promote group creativity. They enable us to develop our creativity patterns in interaction with others. Examples of physical games are tag, dodge ball, and baseball. The physical aspects of these games require the participants to stretch their creative talents and interact with others.

One advantage of physical games is that they have numerous possible outcomes. Many games foster teamwork and group skills. Those who are most creative will always search for more than one solution to a given opportunity.

## Example: Using Physical Games

### Step 1. Define the opportunity.

► We must improve our ability to work together.

### Step 2. Pick a physical game.

► Keep-Away

### Step 3. Use the physical game to help you generate possibilities to approach your opportunity.

► Choose two departments that have conflicts.
► Assign observers. (Managers are good to place in this role.) Have them begin the game of Keep-Away.
► Stop the game after several minutes. Have the observers report what they have observed.
► Relate these observations to what is occurring between the departments in their daily activities. Use this input to develop an approach for improving the way the departments work together.

This same method can also be used to address conflicts among three or more individuals. For example, the accounting department may have very strong individuals who overwhelm shipping. When shipping submits documentation, accounting demands information that is beyond the knowledge or ability of the shipping department to provide.

The physical games approach is best for groups working on personal issues. It uses nonlinear creativity. It is best applied to tasks. The creative power of this tool is best seen when it is applied to short time frames. It provides a way to examine your issues in a group setting.

## Games of Chance

> ### GAMES OF CHANCE
>
> **Type:**  Provoked
> **Issue:**  Planning
> **Who:**  Group
>
> **Step 1.**  Define your opportunity.
>
> **Step 2.**  Pick a game of chance.
>
> **Step 3.**  Use the game of chance to help you generate ways to approach your opportunity.

Games of chance promote the breaking of normal patterns as we interact with others. Some games of chance include dice, cards, and coin tossing.

One advantage of games of chance is that they have many possible outcomes. They ensure that participants consider more than one solution for a given opportunity. Such games allow a group to examine different plans with minimal risk.

## Example: Using Games of Chance

### Step 1. Define the opportunity.

> ▶ We must develop a better method for responding to our customers.

### Step 2. Pick a game of chance.

> ▶ Dice

**Step 3. Use the game of chance to help you generate possibilities to approach your opportunity.**

▶ Roll a pair of dice and record the number (9).

▶ Roll them a second time and multiply the two results ($9 \times 4 = 36$).

▶ Roll them a third time and multiply the result by the new number ($36 \times 5 = 180$).

▶ Look in a dictionary on the page number indicated by the result (180).

▶ Roll five dice and count down the dictionary page to the number indicated (19).

▶ Use the word (*distort*) to develop an approach to developing a better method of responding to the customer. For example, customers often distort a situation. It's very useful, therefore, to develop a consistent set of questions to get the actual details of what is occurring.

Games of chance function best for groups working on enterprise issues. This approach uses provoked creativity. It is best applied to planning. The creative power of this tool is best seen when it is applied to medium time frames. It provides a way to examine your issues in relation to multiple options.

**Games of chance can provoke your creativity and help you decide what to do.**

# Mental Games

## MENTAL GAMES

**Type:**  "Aha"
**Issue:**  Planning
**Who:**  Individual

**Step 1.**  Define your opportunity.

**Step 2.**  Pick a mental game.

**Step 3.**  Use the mental game to help you generate ways to approach your opportunity.

Mental games promote the exploration of beliefs and self-imposed barriers. They are contemplative in nature and enable us to identify our normal patterns. Examples of mental games are What If, Imagineering, and Speculation.

The mental aspects require participants to break their normal patterns as they interact with others. One advantage to mental games is that there are no barriers except those that are self-imposed. Mental games foster a unique examination of what can be. They ensure that participants consider more than one solution for a given opportunity. They are very effective for helping individuals consider broad frontiers.

## Example: Using Mental Games

### Step 1. Define the opportunity.

▶ You must develop a better way to utilize the Internet.

### Step 2. Pick a mental game.

▶ What If

### Step 3. Use the mental game to help you generate possibilities to approach your opportunity.

- ▶ You have been charged with developing a new method of using the Internet. Imagine yourself as Jules Verne.
- ▶ Ask yourself, "What if Jules Verne were faced with having to develop a better way to utilize the Internet?"
- ▶ What if you could project pictures in three dimensions in the middle of the room?
- ▶ What if people could see every nuance, smell every smell, and hear everything going on somewhere else?
- ▶ How would the answers to these questions change your approach to using the Internet? You might start to develop real-time, real-world vacations that could be enjoyed in your own living room.

Mental games function best for individuals working on personal issues. They call on "Aha" creativity. They are best applied to direction setting. The creative power of this tool is best seen when it is applied to long time frames. It provides a way to examine your issues in relation to potential future configurations.

*We see every problem as a nail if our only tool is a hammer.*
    ABRAHAM H. MASLOW

We humans are competitive animals. We like to win; we like to build. To create a winning scenario, we become innovative and can come up with new insights and new ways of doing things.

This learning and growing, this competition, these experiences, these games can take a very mechanical form, as with puzzles, card games, board games, skill games, or computer games. The broad range of games includes

- ▶ Physical games,
- ▶ Mental games,
- ▶ Games that require skill, and
- ▶ Games of chance.

Personal growth comes from academic education, from training, from social experiences, and from the reading and learning we do on our own. An extreme form of experiential learning occurs when one is cut loose in the out-back and asked to maintain oneself with only a blanket and a match. An Outward Bound experience provides a sufficient, if not a traumatic emotional event to unleash new insight and growth. People often see games as fun, as challenge merely for the sake of challenge. To stimulate your own creativity, choose the appropriate game to create the experience that will give you and your teammates the insights that will help you get where you need to go.

Certain games have very formal structures and rules, boards, pieces, and the like. We recommend that you buy popular games such as Scrabble or Monopoly, then change the rules and the wording to reflect your issue. While you are playing Monopoly, you will actually be working on the issues that face your organization. Be willing to change the rules of any game to approach your particular situation more creatively.

# Just for Fun

Which of these shapes is least like the others? Why?

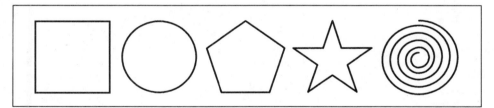

Our logic can be found in Appendix B. Compare it to your answer.

# 14

# Putting It All Together: Overcoming Barriers and Opening Doors

## Innovative Organizations

*Innovative companies:*
*Focus on customer value.*
*Innovate across all their functions and up and down the business system with suppliers and distributors.*
*Do more, faster, and more often.*
   ANDREW J. PARSONS

Creativity is an individual trait. Put creative people together in small groups (departments), and you get originality. Put small groups together into organizations, and you get innovation. That's what Bill Gates has done at Microsoft, becoming the richest man in the world at age 40. In a *Fortune* magazine survey (December 1993) of senior U.S. executives, 39 percent of the respondents indicated that Microsoft was the most innovative organization in the nation. A very distant number two was General Electric, with only 18 percent of the votes. The 10 most innovative organizations in the United States, in order, are shown in the figure.

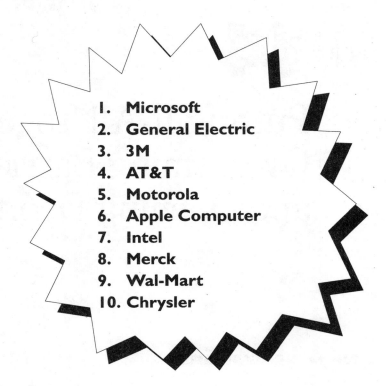

1. Microsoft
2. General Electric
3. 3M
4. AT&T
5. Motorola
6. Apple Computer
7. Intel
8. Merck
9. Wal-Mart
10. Chrysler

What sets these highly innovative organizations apart from the rest? By looking closely at the way these organizations are managed, we see six key elements that are the major contributors to the innovative environment:

► Individuals—their rights and dignity—are respected.
► Aggressive performance-related measurements are applied to everyone and everything.
► Constructive dissatisfaction is encouraged.
► A low level of fear exists throughout the organization.
► Failure is viewed as a learning process.
► Technology is used as an enabler rather than as a driver.

## Constructive Dissatisfaction

Of the six characteristics mentioned, one—constructive dissatisfaction—requires explanation. Most organizations would feel that they were performing poorly if they had dissatisfied employees. We don't agree with that view. Certainly, we do not want employees who are complaining and moaning—that is destructive dissatisfaction. The innovative organization has people who are not satisfied with doing their jobs the same old way. They are always challenging the system, looking for better ways to deliver the same or better desired output. When constructively dissatisfied employees make suggestions, they do not accept answers like these:

- ▶ That's the way it's done here.
- ▶ We tried that years ago and it didn't work.
- ▶ We'll think about that at a later date.
- ▶ The boss wants it done that way.

Constructively dissatisfied employees are the ones who are saying, "Things can be different. There is a better way to do it, and I'm going to find it." Destructively dissatisfied employees state, "Things are bad—everything's fouled up. This place doesn't operate well."

The difference is that constructively dissatisfied employees personally believe that they can make things better. They think there is a better way, and they are committed to finding it. IBM used to call these people "wild ducks." Management, on a whole, doesn't like to manage wild ducks because they challenge management's set pattern. It is much easier to have people snap to attention and say, "Yes, sir. I'll do it your way." As a result, management spends more time clipping the wild ducks' wings than encouraging them to fly. This is unfortunate because it is the wild ducks who will make your organization great. Of course, the wild ducks fail more often than the domesticated ducks. But they are the ones who make the big breakthroughs. Take time to identify these wild ducks, and encourage them to fly out of the comfortable nest that we all sit in.

## Characteristics of Innovative Organizations

Innovative organizations encourage their people to be creative. Such an organization is quick to recognize a new, creative idea and nurture the creative seed, watering and fertilizing it until it is a blooming, fruit-laden tree. You find innovative organizations all around the world—in France, Renault; in Japan, Sony; in the United States, 3M; in Italy, Fiat. These organizations not only employ creative people, but they effectively transform their employees' creative ideas into revolutionary new products. Many organizations are effective at generating new concepts but ineffective at transforming them into valuable products. Texas Instruments is a good example of an organization that has been very creative on the conceptual level but relatively ineffective at transforming its concepts into competitive advantages.

Innovation means doing new things. There is a vast difference between imagining a new story line and transforming the story line into a book. Many people realize this difference quickly when they see someone else come up with a successful new product that they recognize as an idea they had conceived but never done anything with. Creativity without innovation equals lost opportunities and discouragement.

The simple graph displayed on the computer screen in the figure shows the relationship between risk and degree of creativity. Note that the bottom axis represents a continuum from very creative to traditional. (The typical lowest-to-highest continuum is reversed so the relationship between creativity and risk can be represented.)

The organization that combines creativity and innovation has a significant competitive advantage. The truly creative organization looks at the concept development process and the related risks in a unique way, as shown on the computer screen. In such an organization, concepts evolve through five distinct steps.

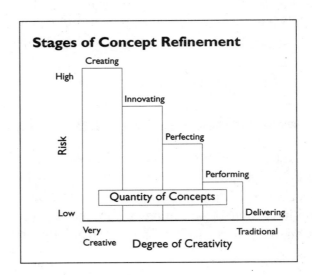

### Step 1. Creating

**Highest Risk**
**Highest**
**Creativity**

During the creating step, the organization is willing to accept a very high risk that a particular idea or concept will not be practical or usable. It is understood and expected that a high percentage of these concepts will fail. But in reality, are those instances failures, or are they negative successes? As one pro football player stated, "I tackle everybody in sight and just throw away the ones who don't have the ball." You should not be discouraged if you fail. Remember—in baseball, you can fail two out of three times at the plate and still earn a multimillion-dollar salary. A batting average of .333 is very good.

### Step 2. Innovating

**High Risk**
**High**
**Creativity**

During the innovating step, there still is a high risk that the concept may not be usable or practical. For example, Thomas A. Edison, while trying to develop the electric light bulb, was asked by a reporter if he were discouraged because he had tried so many different combinations and all of them had failed. Edison responded that he had not failed; rather, he had discovered a number of materials that were not candidates for the electric light bulb filament.

### Step 3. Perfecting

**Moderate**
**Risk**
**Moderate**
**Creativity**

At the perfecting step, the risk that the concept will be unusable is greatly reduced, and plans are developed to market the product.

### Step 4. Performing

**Low Risk**
**Low**
**Creativity**

Once the concept is perfected, the organization moves into the performing stage, establishing capabilities to meet customer requirements and quantities. Risk of the concept failing at this point should be very low.

### Step 5. Delivering

**Lowest Risk**
**Lowest**
**Creativity**

By the time the organization enters the stage of delivering to internal and/or external customers, the risk related to concept failure should be minimal or nonexistent.

*Failure is only the opportunity to more intelligently begin again.*
HENRY FORD

# Integrated Organizations

Organizations that have effectively integrated creativity and innovation function differently from other organizations. They are willing to take appropriate risks and exhibit the following characteristics:

- ▶ Noble failures are accepted as learning experiences, not as career-jeopardizing experiences.
- ▶ Creativity is encouraged and practiced in all departments, not just in Research and Development.
- ▶ Suggestion programs are given high priority; suggestions are answered in hours or days, not months.
- ▶ Formal creativity recognition systems are established and function well.
- ▶ Creativity is a prime consideration in promotions.
- ▶ Managers are compensated and rated on the basis of the numbers of creative items implemented as a result of their teams' work.
- ▶ Management accepts high initial risks, but management systems ensure that the risks are eliminated or minimized before the concept is delivered to external or internal customers.
- ▶ Risk management training is widely used at all levels, and the methodologies are utilized effectively.
- ▶ Fast-track systems are in place to recognize and move concepts through the process that has significant impact on the organization.
- ▶ Current approaches are always being questioned.
- ▶ There is a well-defined process to transform creative ideas into reality at minimum cost and cycle time.
- ▶ Senior management meets regularly with employees at all levels to elicit their suggestions and concerns.
- ▶ Change is seen as an opportunity, not a threat.
- ▶ The focus is on "What's new" rather than "How many."
- ▶ Time is budgeted within every job for the creativity process.

▶ Management employs a particular language to talk about the business, often using phrases like "Let's be radical" or "Why do you think that's impractical?" Management's job is to transform the impractical concept into a business opportunity.

▶ Individuals who generate and implement new ideas are publicly recognized. Creativity training is considered part of job training.

▶ Open communication channels are maintained, providing everyone with information regarding the needs of the organization and its customers.

▶ Budgets are structured to make available risk money for evaluating new concepts that are not part of the yearly business plan.

▶ Town meeting–style get-togethers are held frequently to encourage people to discuss issues and share concepts.

## Key Approaches Used by Creative Organizations

The following baker's dozen key approaches define the environment that an organization must develop to tap its full creative powers.

▶ Encourage risk taking by eliminating the fear of failure. Accept noble failures as learning experiences.

▶ Establish a direct correlation between creative and innovative output of individuals and natural work groups and the reward structure.

▶ Communicate openly the organization's business strategy, challenges, and direction.

▶ Have a well-defined and documented concept development cycle that includes a fast track to expedite the processing of exceptional ideas.

▶ Provide creativity training to all employees, and give them time to exercise their creativity.

▶ Set creativity goals for all natural work groups and managers.

▶ Create a sense of urgency. The organization should be frustrated if major changes are not under way. Establish procedures for managing change and chaos.

▶ Eliminate the copycat mentality. The organization should stop copying the competition. It should aim to be the leader, not the biggest in the industry. Benchmarking can be detrimental because it tends to make the organization a follower, not a leader. However, competitive comparisons are helpful in understanding how the organization is progressing in relation to the competition.

▶ Take a balanced approach to creativity: There is a balance between applying the organization's creative skills to problems and applying it to new opportunities.

▶ Set innovative priorities based on an idea's potential value to the organization, and measure the results. Do not base priorities on the novelty of the idea.

▶ Have a good understanding of when to halt the creative and innovative processes and when to begin the perfecting process.

▶ Communicate large and small examples of creative and innovative success to the entire organization.

▶ Make creativity and innovation a fun part of everyone's job.

*If you're not failing every now and again, it's a sign you're not doing anything very innovative.*
ANDREW J. PARSONS

# Do Something with It

Ideas generated in organizations sometimes result in breakthroughs in implementation. Often, however, creative ideas result in heartache, frustration, and disappointment. One reason for this outcome is that ideas basically start with individuals—they come from human minds. A creative insight can produce an idea that either has or does not have merit. Either it is good, or it is not good. It is either effective or ineffective in the current situation. Either it is going to work, or it is not going to work. It would be impossible to find a macro statistic for all the trillions of ideas that all the billions of people have generated, but truly good ideas are in the minority.

In our experience, we have found that 30 percent of the ideas that are generated have merit and should be implemented. The remaining 70 percent lead down dead-end streets. Consider the classic story of Edison trying to find a filament for incandescent light: After trying 1,200 different filaments, he still had not achieved success. That means 1,200 failures against one success. Our assumption is that 30 percent of ideas have merit and should be implemented.

An organization presents a series of filters in the form of reviews, management checkpoints, budget concerns, and so on, that allow only a certain number of changes, ideas, or creative insights to be implemented within any given time frame. Of the 30 percent good ideas, perhaps 10 percent are implemented (3 percent) and 90 percent are not. Some of the 70 percent bad ideas sneak through. Our experience has shown that of the bad ideas, at least 3 percent of the 70 percent are indeed implemented (2 percent), and 98 percent are not.

According to this scenario, of five ideas that are implemented, 60 percent (3/5) are good ideas and 40 percent (2/5) are bad ideas. This also means that only 5 percent of our ideas are usually implemented (100% − 2% good ideas and 5% bad ideas). Of the 95 percent of the ideas that are not implemented, 27 percent are good ideas that should have been implemented (% good ideas 30% × % good ideas not implemented 10% = 27%). Of the bad ideas, 68 percent were also not implemented (% bad ideas 70% × % bad ideas not implemented 97% = 68%).

---

**Ideas That Get Implemented**

30% Good Ideas
  10% Good Ideas Implemented
    3% of total are good ideas that get implemented
    27% of total are good ideas that don't get implemented

70% Bad Ideas
  3% Bad Ideas Implemented
   2% of total are bad ideas that get implemented
   68% of total are bad ideas that don't get implemented

---

It is easy to see that by far the highest percentage of unused ideas comprises bad ideas. In order for the organization to increase the number of good ideas implemented, it also must risk increasing the number of bad ideas that are implemented. Although some of the tools that we have presented here will help the organization improve its odds of implementing a higher percentage of its good ideas, there will still be a higher number of bad ideas that escape through the system.

This becomes a major reason for an organization to create a climate in which there is freedom to fail, it is okay to come up with something that does not work, and individuals have the liberty to explore new insights and new ways of doing things. There is much more to creative insights than achieving them. For insights to be practical and meaningful, there must be a context or a frame of reference that enables the organization to see the value of good ideas, to support them, and to encourage formatted work spaces where individuals can experiment without jeopardizing their own careers or the entire organization.

William Gore, the late founder of Gore Industries, was fond of telling his engineers that they were in charge of the fate of their organization. He would say, "Imagine us being on a ship at sea. You have a drill. You can drill holes in the hull and look out and see new ideas, just as long as you do not drill below the water line and threaten the organization itself."

We all need that sense of purpose, that empowerment to understand that we control our own destinies and that our success or failure is based on the ability to try new things. We must learn to get up when we trip and fall. The ultimate failure of creativity is not getting up and trying again.

*Problems are only opportunities in work clothes.*
HENRY J. KAISER

## The CEO Innovative Mind-Set Test

Whether you have actively and formally worked toward establishing an innovative mind-set without your organization, you personally may be closer—or farther—from an innovative mind-set than you think. To find out, take the following test, answering Yes or No to each question. For a "Yes" answer, check the box beside the question. For a "No" answer, leave the box blank.

☐ Do I currently incorporate innovation into our business plan as a strategic lever for increasing satisfaction among shareholders, employees, and customers?

☐ Have I consciously used innovation and launched new products to help boost my company's stock price or increase my company's value?

☐ Have I purposely developed a balanced portfolio of new product types entailing varying degrees of risk, ranging from radically new to the world to line extensions and repositioning?

☐ Do I teach my management team to view innovation as an investment opportunity rather than as a cost center that negatively affects quarterly earnings?

☐ Do I have in place a commonly agreed upon innovation strategy that links the role of innovation and new products to our business strategy?

☐ Have I made innovation an attractive career path for employees to pursue?

☐ Do I regularly celebrate new product failures with as much fervor as new product successes with all team members?

☐ Do I uniformly communicate and act in ways that clearly convey trust in the cross-functional teams that are activating innovation?

☐ Do I stimulate an entrepreneurial environment by having in place a performance-based compensation system for new-product participants?

☐ Do I measure and communicate throughout the organization the return on innovation for our company?

☐ Do I really know how much innovation costs, and do I set realistic return expectations for innovation?

☐ Do I provide "ceilingless" and motivating compensation rewards to new-product participants and allow them to invest in the new products they are developing?

☐ Do I select the best people within the company (i.e., those whom I feel I cannot afford to divert from existing business) to activate the new-product process?

☐ Do I make sure we conduct consumer research to identify problems and needs before we embark on idea generation?

☐ Do I ensure that idea generation is a problem-solving endeavor aimed at generating potential solutions to address consumer needs?

☐ Do I maintain funding and resource allocation for innovation at a consistent level, rather than pulling the plug after a "down" quarter?

☐ Do I truly accept that 40 percent to 50 percent of future new-product launches will fail?

☐ Do all R&D people get at least 15 percent "free time" (unassigned to any specific project) to have breathing space and the freedom to explore their own ideas?

☐ Do I have a well-articulated technology strategy that defines technology platforms and areas of needed technical expertise to help support the innovation initiatives?

☐ Do I hear others throughout the organization talk about my positive, enthusiastic, supportive, and "can-do" attitude toward innovation?

### Scoring

☐ Total number of "Yes" answers

Give yourself five points for each "Yes" answer.
Total "Yes" × 5 = _____.

- ▶ 80 and over—OUTSTANDING. You already have a strong innovation mind-set.
- ▶ 60 to 79—GOOD. You are evolving toward an innovative mind-set.
- ▶ Under 60—You have a negative mind-set toward innovation.

# Some Common Barriers

Overcoming the barriers to creativity is critical to your success. We will address some of the more common barriers. It is up to you to develop your own best method to overcome each barrier.

### Barrier 1. Mismatching the tool and the method with the expected outcome.

A classic manifestation of this barrier is putting people in a room and telling them to come up with any ideas they want, on the assumption that they will be able to redefine the nature of the organization and ensure expected outcomes, such as higher profits and new markets. Another manifestation is the opposite: Putting senior people in a room and telling them to determine their strategy for the next decade through formal numerical analysis and a very logical set of tools. The limitations inhibit their creative strategic thinking.

### Barrier 2. Expecting everyone in the organization to engage in exactly the same kind of creativity.

The creativity styles and methods of all 50,000 people in an organization will not be consistent with either the circumstance or the available skills. Different tools are appropriate for addressing different kinds of issues using different styles of creativity.

### Barrier 3. Believing that creativity on demand will work every time.

This barrier is the assumption that you need only tell people to be creative, and they will find a new and better way. Spontaneous creativity has its place, as does formal creativity. Cutting people loose with no definition of creativity, no understanding of its nature, and no training or practice in being creative inhibits their creative abilities.

### Barrier 4. Thinking that being creative is enough to guarantee success.

Creativity alone—like efficiency, effectiveness, or adaptability alone—is not sufficient to ensure success. Indeed, all four of those key factors exist within some conceptual frame of reference. The good news is that if you understand the frame of reference, you can then optimize your allocation of resources toward efficiency, effectiveness, creativity, and adaptability. The bad news is that the frame of reference changes continually, and the ultimate creative challenge for anyone is to understand the new frame of reference, the dynamic context.

There is a wide choice of tools for creativity. The difficulty is not a lack of tools but a lack of appropriate application of the tools. Before choosing and using tools, understand what you are trying to accomplish.

Creativity cannot be provided on demand. However, there are numerous methodologies, tools, and techniques that can help. Remember the following points:

- ▶ 80 percent of creative breakthroughs are brought about by 20 percent of the tools.
- ▶ You must choose the method that is appropriate for you.
- ▶ Creativity methods can be used in any order.
- ▶ Creativity methods can be used more than once to address a given issue.
- ▶ Addressing a given issue may require several different approaches and methods.
- ▶ Simple methods are best.
- ▶ Either group or individual efforts can be fruitful in achieving creativity. The determining factor is the context in which the method is being applied.
- ▶ This book has been designed so that you do not have to read the entire text to use the tools.
- ▶ Each tool, each method stands alone.

## Just for Fun

Move two adjacent coins at the same time. First, move two coins to one end. Each additional move requires that you move two coins into the vacant space. The objective is to have four black coins and four white coins in a row. Either black or white may come first. What is the smallest possible number of moves? What are the moves?

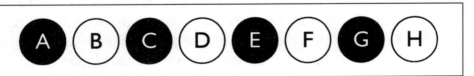

One solution is in Appendix B.

# APPENDIX |  A

# Tool Summary

In this appendix we have summarized all the individual creativity improvement tools and techniques outlined in this book. We hope this ready reference will help you find the right approach for each occasion.

    The number at the right-hand corner of each chart is the page in the book where the approach is discussed. In the lower left-hand corner of the chart, you will find a *G* or an *I*. *G* indicates that the tool is best used by a group of people; *I* indicates that it is best used by an individual.

## Mind Expanders

### The Two-Minute Mind
*page 56*

Step 1:    Sit in front of a clock with a sweep second hand.

Step 2:    Concentrate only on the second hand for two minutes.

Step 3:    If you lose concentration, start over again.

*I*

### Mindbeats
*page 56*

Step 1:    Sit in a quiet place with a pencil and a blank piece of paper.

Step 2:    For three minutes, slowly draw a straight horizontal line, concentrating on the point of the pencil.

Step 3:    Each time your concentration drifts away from the pencil point, draw a mindbeat.

*I*

### The Alphabet
*page 57*

Step 1:    Think about the alphabet.

Step 2:    Count the number of capital letters that have curved lines in them.

Step 3:    Count the number of small letters that have straight lines in them.

*I*

## The Numbers

Step 1:     Recite the even numbers from 2 to 100.
Step 2:     Recite the even numbers from 100 to 2.
Step 3:     Repeat Steps 1 and 2, but go up or down by multiples of 3.
Step 4:     Do Step 3 for the multiples of all numbers from 4 to 9.

*I*

## A Nursery Rhyme

Step 1:     Memorize the verse "Mary Had a Little Lamb."
Step 2:     Recite the verse, numbering each word.
Step 3:     Recite the verse, saying the number of letters in the word before each word.

*I*

## Common Objects

Step 1:     Select two objects on your desk.
Step 2:     Study them for a minute.
Step 3:     Write down two or three ways that they could be changed to become more effective.

*I*

## Personal Creativity

Step 1:     List two of your best creative ideas that have been implemented.
Step 2:     List three things you can do to become more creative at work.
Step 3:     List three things you can do to become more creative at home.

*I*

## Analyzing Outrageous Ideas

Step 1:     Keep a piece of paper with you so that you can write down every outrageous idea that you don't put to use.
Step 2:     Review the list at the end of the day, putting check marks in front of the ideas that should not have been rejected.
Step 3:     Write down why you rejected them.
Step 4:     Select three to six of the ideas that you still believe are bad, listing what was good about the ideas and how they could be reshaped into acceptable concepts.

*I*

## Pictures to Drive Creativity *page 59*

Step 1: Look at some magazines and cut out an interesting variety of pictures of people and situations that evoke ambiguities.

Step 2: Select three or four pictures at random.

Step 3: Create a story that includes the items in the pictures.

*I*

---

## Words to Drive Creativity *page 60*

Step 1: Write down interesting nouns on separate cards.

Step 2: Pull three to five cards at random from the pile.

Step 3: Make up a story using the nouns on those cards.

*I*

---

## Differences and Similarities *page 61*

Step 1: Shuffle the cards from "Words to Drive Creativity."

Step 2: Pull out two cards at random.

Step 3: Make a list of ways the items are the same and ways they are different.

*I*

---

## Defining Other Applications *page 61*

Step 1: Select a card at random from "Words to Drive Creativity."

Step 2: Ask yourself how the item is normally used.

Step 3: Ask yourself how the item can be used differently.

*I*

---

## Creative Progress Reports *page 62*

Step 1: At the end of the week, prepare a progress report on a three-by-five card.

Step 2: On the top half, write what you did during the week.

Step 3: On the bottom half, write what you accomplished.

Step 4: On the back, write how you feel about your job and how you feel about what you accomplished.

Step 5: Write a statement of what you will do the following week to make things better.

*I*

---

### Dreaming in Color                                        *page 63*

Step 1:   Buy a selection of bright-colored paper.

Step 2:   Just before you go to bed, study one of the colored pages intensely for five minutes.

Step 3:   Turn off the light, and try to visualize the color in your mind for the next five minutes.

Step 4:   Each night, use a different color.

Step 5:   Once you are competent at visualizing colors, move on to patterns.

*I*

### Recording Your Evening's Activities                      *page 64*

Step 1:   Keep a pad and pencil beside your bed to record ideas that come to you during the night.

Step 2:   Whenever an idea occurs, record it right away.

Step 3:   Keep a graph that records the number of creative ideas you have per week.

*I*

### Discarding the Boombox                                   *page 65*

Step 1:   Select songs with rich instrumental accompaniments.

Step 2:   Set up your stereo to play the same combination of songs over and over for 30 minutes a day.

Step 3:   Make a tape on which you record every other song, leaving blank spaces for the songs that are missing.

Step 4:   Mentally fill in the blank spaces.

Step 5:   Think of a vocalist singing one of his or her most famous songs.

Step 6:   Think of that vocalist singing one of your recorded songs.

*I*

## Creativity Tools

### Brainstorming                                            *page 99*

Step 1:   Select a purpose for the brainstorming session. Be as specific as possible, but consider the resources available to the group.

Step 2:   Review the rules of brainstorming.

Step 3:   Generate ideas.

*G*

### Card Sort/Affinity Diagram                                    *page 111*

Step 1:   Define the opportunity, problem, or situation in very broad terms.
          Word the definition clearly.
Step 2:   Generate ideas using brainstorming.
Step 3:   Sort the idea cards into groups
Step 4:   Generate header cards.

G

### Cards and Games                                              *page 132*

Step 1:   Determine in what area creative breakthrough is required.
Step 2:   Acquire the appropriate card set or game.
Step 3:   Assemble the right group if required.
Step 4:   Use the card deck or game as a mechanism to change the paradigm in which you function.

G

### Cartoon Drawing                                              *page 91*

Step 1:   Define the opportunity, problem, or situation.
Step 2:   Use an existing cartoon with the words and titles removed, or draw a new cartoon figure that seems to capture something about the opportunity, problem, or situation.
Step 3:   Develop new captions.
Step 4:   Debrief the session, focusing on new insights and learnings.

I

### Code Talk                                                    *page 102*

Step 1:   Describe the opportunity, problem, or situation.
Step 2:   Develop a different way to describe the opportunity, problem, or situation, such as in terms of a garden, zoo, or circus.
Step 3:   Analyze your description for new insights.
Step 4:   Develop more than one solution based on your new insights.

G

## Conversation

*page 134*

Step 1: Engage in conversation with others, preferably people who do not share your viewpoint and background.

Step 2: Listen to what is said.

Step 3: Apply what is said to your own situation.

*I*

## Drawing

*page 141*

Step 1: Determine the process or product to be studied.

Step 2: Draw your issue as something else or from a different perspective.

Step 3: Explain your drawing.

*I*

## Environment

*page 120*

Step 1: Determine the type of creativity you are going to use.

Step 2: Set up your environment to improve your creativity.

Step 3: Remember what works and what doesn't.

*I*

## Exaggerated Objectives

*page 75*

Step 1: Define the opportunity.

Step 2: List the criteria that will satisfy the opportunity.

Step 3: Exaggerate the criteria.

Step 4: Use the exaggerated criteria to generate ideas.

*G*

## Five "Whys"

*page 124*

Step 1: Ask "Why" in relation to an opportunity, problem, or situation.

Step 2: Ask "Why" in relation to the answer to the first "Why."

Step 3: Ask "Why" in relation to the answer to the second "Why."

Step 4: Ask "Why" in relation to the answer to the third "Why."

Step 5: Ask "Why" in relation to the answer to the fourth "Why."

Step 6: Continue this process until you reach a point where a creative idea or solution is possible.

*G*

## Force Analysis

*page 108*

Step 1:  Define your opportunity, problem, or situation.
Step 2:  Draw a large circle.
Step 3:  Define or describe what is preventing you from succeeding (restraining forces).
Step 4:  Define or describe why you need to succeed (driving forces).
Step 5:  Analyze each of the forces.

*G*

## Free Association

*page 104*

Step 1:  Get out of your normal environment.
Step 2:  Pick any item, word, idea, or concept.
Step 3:  Freely associate this idea with something else.
Step 4:  Continue to build on the ideas as they are developed until you have exhausted your possibilities or you have experienced an "Aha."

*I*

## Games of Chance

*page 175*

Step 1:  Define your opportunity.
Step 2:  Pick a game of chance.
Step 3:  Use the game of chance to help you generate possibilities to approach your opportunity.

*G*

## Listening for Comprehension

*page 93*

Step 1:  Hear all of the words that are spoken.
Step 2:  Seek the logic behind the words.
Step 3:  Determine the motivation behind the logic.
Step 4:  Understand the feelings behind the motivation.
Step 5:  Frame your understanding in your own words.

*I*

## Manager to Manager Event
*page 79*

Step 1:    Hold work unit workshop.
Step 2:    Have unit manager's manager sit behind unit manager.
Step 3:    Unit presents recommendations.
Step 4:    Manager makes yes/no or specific date decision.
G

## Measles Chart
*page 143*

Step 1:    Determine the process or product to be studied.
Step 2:    Draw a diagram of the product or process.
Step 3:    Mark errors on the diagram where they occur.
Step 4:    Analyze the results.
G

## Mental Games
*page 177*

Step 1:    Define your opportunity.
Step 2:    Pick a mental game.
Step 3:    Use the mental game to help you generate ways to approach your opportunity.
I

## Mind Mapping
*page 115*

Step 1:    Define the topic.
Step 2:    Draw a central image of the topic.
Step 3:    Record related images around the central image.
Step 4:    Follow the same technique for each of the new images.
Step 5:    Expand images as long as your creativity continues.
Step 6:    Group together ideas that have common themes.
I

## Musts/Wants/Wows
*page 164*

Step 1:    Define your target.
Step 2:    Create a matrix.
Step 3:    Generate a list of needs, sort the list of needs into levels, and load the needs into the matrix.
G

## Partitioning

*page 150*

Step 1:    Define the problem or opportunity.
Step 2:    Divide it into the elements that make up your cultural frame of reference.
Step 3:    Divide these elements into underlying assumptions.
Step 4:    Develop a solution to overcome the assumptions.
*G*

## Physical Games

*page 173*

Step 1:    Define your opportunity.
Step 2:    Pick a physical game.
Step 3:    Use the physical game to help you generate possibilities to approach your opportunity.
*G*

## Physical Models

*page 167*

Step 1:    Define the situation.
Step 2:    Develop a model of the situation using physical pieces and parts.
*G*

## Pick-Up Sticks

*page 168*

Step 1:    Define each stick as a force that impacts you.
Step 2:    Define your position in relation to the force.
Step 3:    Examine the interactions between this force and others that impact you.
*I*

## Polar Cases

*page 166*

Step 1:    Define the situation.
Step 2:    Define the best and worst cases for the situation.
Step 3:    Determine what you must do to achieve the best case and avoid the worst case.
*I*

## Possibility Generator

*page 77*

Step 1:   Define the objective.

Step 2:   Break each element into subelements.

Step 3:   Combine subelements into any new ideas that come to mind.

Step 4:   Evaluate your new options, using the selection window to help you decide which you should pursue.

*G*

## Presentation

*page 155*

Step 1:   Develop your presentation.

Step 2:   Practice.

Step 3:   Introduce your subject. Present your work. Conclude with a summary. Allow opportunity for questions. Ask for assistance if required.

*G*

## Rainbow Flow Charting

*page 138*

Step 1:   Determine the process or product to be studied.

Step 2:   Draw a diagram of the product or process using symbols and colors.

Step 3:   Describe how the process does or should work by placing descriptions in the symbols.

Step 4:   Analyze the differences between what is and what should be.

*G*

## Reality Matrix

*page 153*

Step 1:   Define the steps of the process.

Step 2:   Define who is responsible for each step.

Step 3:   Define when each step will be done.

Step 4:   Analyze for missing steps and completion times.

*G*

### Role-Playing

*page 89*

Step 1:     Define the opportunity, problem, or situation.
Step 2:     Define who is or should be involved.
Step 3:     Assign a role to each individual.
Step 4:     Role-play.
Step 5:     Debrief the session, focusing on new insights and learnings.

*G*

---

### Say/Think

*page 86*

Step 1:     Draw three columns on a pad.
Step 2:     Record what is said in a conversation and by whom it is said.
Step 3:     Write down what you were thinking after each statement.
Step 4:     Review what was said and what you thought. If you trust the person(s) with whom you had the conversation, share your written thoughts.

*G*

---

### Selection Window

*page 71*

Step 1:     Develop a list of ideas.
Step 2:     Give each idea a score for each criterion.
Step 3:     Place the ideas into the selection window.
Step 4:     Analyze and do.

*I*

---

### Service Ladder

*page 145*

Step 1:     Define the process to examine.
Step 2:     Map the waiting and working times.
Step 3:     Analyze where waiting time can be eliminated.

*G*

---

### Skill Games

*page 172*

Step 1:     Define your opportunity.
Step 2:     Pick a skill game.
Step 3:     Use the skill game to help you generate possibilities to approach your opportunity.

*I*

---

### Song Titles
*page 98*

Step 1:    Define the opportunity, problem, or situation.

Step 2:    Think of an appropriate song, TV show, or movie title that describes it.

Step 3:    Explain why the song, TV show, or movie title is appropriate.

*I*

---

### Thinking Words
*page 127*

Step 1:    Isolate the opportunity, problem, or situation you want to think about.

Step 2:    Ask CREATES questions about each stage of the opportunity, problem, or situation, and see what ideas emerge.

*G*

---

### Tour
*page 157*

Step 1:    Determine the type of tour.

Step 2:    Go—observe.

Step 3:    Apply learnings to your environment.

*I*

---

# Answers to "Just for Fun"

### Foreword

Answer to the damaged oil pan problem:

She shredded a bar of PGE yellow hard soap and put it in water to soften it. She then pushed it into the hole in the oil pan and let it dry. Before it completely hardened, she turned over the engine to give the piston rod clearance and to pack the soap against the inside of the oil pan. When it was dry, it was so hard that you couldn't put your fingernail into it. She then filled the car with motorboat oil (the only type of oil she had). Obviously, she was far more creative than my two fishing buddies and I, even though all of us were engineers at IBM.

### Chapter 1

One solution is shown here. The authors know that there are many more solutions. They have seen at least 20.

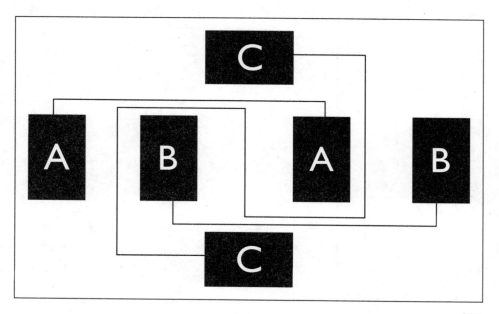

### Chapter 2

This is one solution. Can you add another match and still touch all of the other matches?

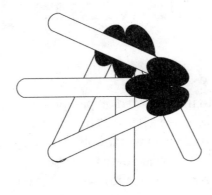

### Chapter 3

The horizontal and vertical lines are the same length.

### Chapter 4

Here is our solution.

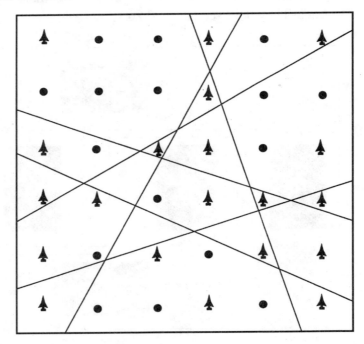

## Chapter 5

The circles are the same size.

## Chapter 6

The horizontal lines are the same length.

## Chapter 7

The diagonal lines are parallel.

## Chapter 8

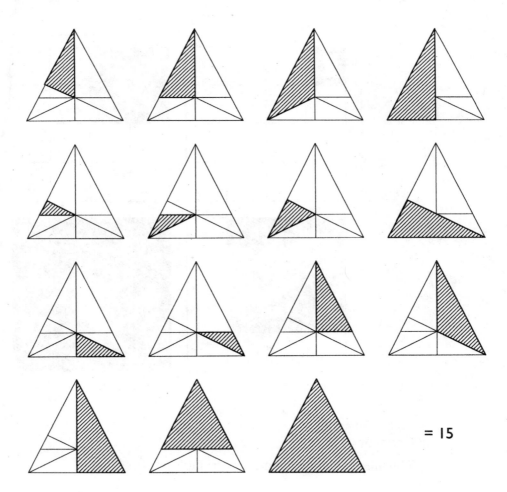

= 15

## Chapter 9

Either six or seven, depending on whether you see the top or the bottom of the box as black.

## Chapter 10

There are numerous answers to this question. If you define a box as having four sides, a top, and a bottom, then there may or may not be boxes. This could be a top view. Furthermore, a box may or may not be square. If this is a top view of boxes that are square, here is a solution. What would the answer be if this were the top view of a group of boxes that could be squares or rectangles?

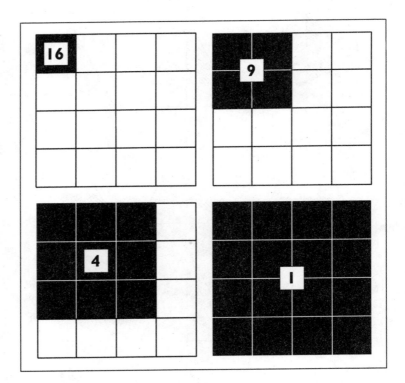

## Chapter 11

The lines in the square and the triangle are straight.

## Chapter 12

This is one of many possible solutions.

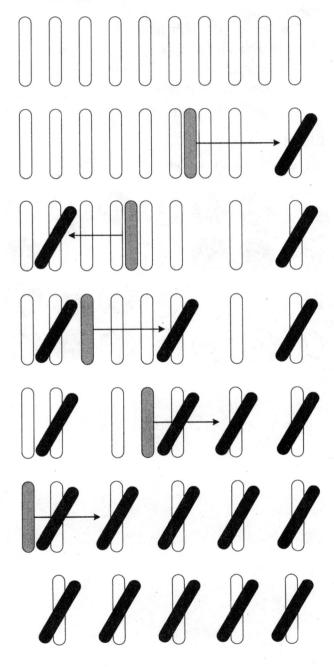

### Chapter 13

Any answer is acceptable. Each has its own unique characteristics. For instance:

The square: Has only four sides.
The circle: Has no corners and no beginning or end.
The polygon: Has only 5 points.
The star: Has 10 points.
The spiral: Has a beginning and an end.

### Chapter 14

One solution is shown here.

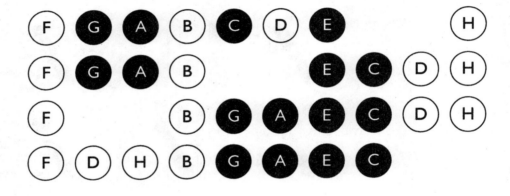

# Bibliography

Buzan, Tony, *Use Both Sides of Your Brain,* 3rd ed. New York: A Plume Book, 1991.

Caroselli, Marlene, *Breakthrough Creativity. Developing Ideas That Make a Difference.* White Plains, NY: Quality Resources, 1994.

de Bono, Edward, *Lateral Thinking Creativity Step by Step.* New York: Harper & Row, 1970.

de Bono, Edward, *Serious Creativity. Using the Power of Lateral Thinking to Create New Ideas.* HarperBusiness, 1992.

Gouillart, Francis J., and James N. Kelly, *Transforming the Organization. Reframing Corporate Direction, Restructuring the Company, Revitalizing the Enterprise, Renewing People.* New York: McGraw-Hill, 1995.

Harp, David, *The New Three-Minute Meditator.*

Higgins, James M., *101 Creative Problem Solving Techniques: The Handbook of New Ideas for Business.* Winter Park, FL: The New Management Publishing Company, 1994.

Hoffherr, Glen D., *The Toolbook. Decision Making and Planning for Optimum Results.* Windham, NH: Markon Inc., 1993.

Hoffherr, Glen D., John Moran, and Jerry Nadler, *Breakthrough Thinking in Total Quality Management.* Englewood Cliffs, NJ: Prentice Hall, 1994.

Illig, David, *Learning to Relax—Subliminal Motivation.* New York: Metacon, 1993.

Kravette, Steve, *Complete Meditation.*

Kuczmarski, Thomas D., *Innovation: Leadership Strategies for the Competitive Edge.* New York: NTC Business Books, 1996.

Michalko, Michael, *Thinkertoys: A Handbook of Business Creativity for the 90s.* Berkeley, CA: Ten Speed Press, 1991.

Mignosa, Charles P., *Melting Your Cares Away.* San Jose, CA: Mignosa Associates.

Redfield, Salle Merrill, *The Joy of Meditating: A Beginner's Guide to the Art of Meditation.*

Scannell, Edward E., and John W. Newstrom, *More Games Trainers Play.* New York: McGraw-Hill, 1983.

Tapscott, Don, and Art Caston, *Paradigm Shift. The New Promise of Information Technology.* New York: McGraw-Hill, 1993.

VanGundy, Arthur B., *Idea Power Techniques & Resources to Unleash the Creativity in Your Organization.* New York: American Management Association, 1992.

von Oech, Roger, *A Whack on the Side of the Head. How You Can Be More Creative,* rev. ed. Stanford, CT: U.S. Games Systems, Inc., 1990.

Workshops of Thiagi, *Games, Etc. How to Improve Learning, Performance, and Productivity.* Englewood Cliffs, NJ: Educational Technology Publications, Inc., 1980.

# Glossary

**Cause-and-effect diagrams**   Sometimes known as fish-bone diagrams. They portray the relationship between a problem and its possible causes, providing an opportunity for graphically developing, exploring, and analyzing the relationship.

**Change**   A condition in which an individual's expectations are no longer aligned with the environment. Change occurs when expectations are not met.

**Fact**   Something that is known with certainty and has been objectively verified.

**Force field analysis**   A technique in which an estimate is made about how good or bad a situation is, then the restraining forces and driving forces are defined and pictured as arrows pointing in the appropriate directions.

**Formatted work space**   A place that is conducive to innovative thinking.

**Hollow rhetoric**   A lot of words that do not amount to much.

**Information**   A random collection of material, constrained and narrower in scope than knowledge and lacking orderly synthesis.

**Innovation**   The act of converting a creative concept or idea into an output.

**Knowledge**   The intellectual, mental components acquired and retained through study and experience.

**Knowledge database**   The aggregate of both true and false information.

**Malicious obedience**   A situation in which, if a supervisor tells a worker to do something that the worker knows is wrong, and the worker follows orders and damage results, the worker can be fired.

**Mindbeat**   A means to develop a visual image that shows changes in concentration levels.

**Mind expanders**   Exercises or approaches that help the individual or team to think differently and more creatively.

**Prework**   Preparation made before the start of a group session for generating ideas.

**Radar chart**   Also called a spider chart. Used to compare two or more items on a number (4 to 12) of different parameters.

**Situation**   Anything that requires a response. It can be a problem that needs to be solved, a choice between options, or a simple need to make a verbal response.

**Status quo**   A condition in which the environment and the individual's expectations about the environment are in harmony. It does not mean that the individual's expectations are being met.

**Structure**   The way a session itself is conducted.

**True**   Exactly conforming to a rule, standard, or pattern.

**Wisdom**   An understanding of what is true, right, or lasting. It involves sound judgment and the ability to apply what has been acquired mentally to the conduct of one's affairs.

**Wisdom database**   A subset of the knowledge database, containing only true information.

# Index

## ERNST & YOUNG LLP/SYSTEMCORP INC.

# GUIDED TOUR

Included with this book is Ernst & Young LLP's/SystemCorp Inc.'s Multimedia Guided Tour CDROM called "Creativity Suspenders" and some other related information.

**System Requirements:**
- Windows 3.1 or higher
- Sound Blaster or comparable sound card
- CDROM Drive
- 8MB RAM
- 4MB free disk space
- 265 color video display adapter

**Installation Instructions:**
1. Start Windows.
2. Load Guided Tour CD into CDROM drive.
3. Select Run from the File or Start menu.
4. Type in **<drive>:\setup** where **<drive>** is the drive letter of your CDROM drive.
5. Follow instructions given in setup program.

## CONTENTS OF CDROM GUIDED TOUR

1. **Multimedia overview of this book**

2. **Relaxation Program prepared by Charles P. Mignosa**

3. **Author's biographies**

4. **Other books in the series**

## ANY QUESTIONS?

If you need any technical assistance or more detailed product information on any of the programs demonstrated, contact **SystemCorp** at 514-339-1067.
Fax in a copy of this page to get a 10% discount on any of our products.

## SOFTWARE AND INFORMATION LICENSE

The software and information on this CD ROM (collectively referred to as the "Product") are the property of The McGraw-Hill Companies, Inc. ("McGraw-Hill") and are protected by both United States copyright law and international copyright treaty provision. You must treat this Product just like a book, except that you may copy it into a computer to be used and you may make archival copies of the Products for the sole purpose of backing up our software and protecting your investment from loss.

By saying "just like a book," McGraw-Hill means, for example, that the Product may be used by any number of people and may be freely moved from one computer location to another, so long as there is no possibility of the Product (or any part of the Product) being used at one location or on one computer while it is being used at another. Just as a book cannot be read by two different people in two different places at the same time (unless, of course, McGraw-Hill's rights are being violated).

McGraw-Hill reserves the right to alter or modify the contents of the Product at any time.

This agreement is effective until terminated. The Agreement will terminate automatically without notice if you fail to comply with any provision of this Agreement. In the event of termination by reason of your breach, you will destroy or erase all copies of the Product installed on any computer system or made for backup purposes and shall expunge the Product from your data storage facilities.

## LIMITED WARRANTY

McGraw-Hill warrants the physical CD ROM(s) enclosed herein to be free of defects in materials and workmanship for a period of sixty days from the purchase date. If McGraw-Hill receives written notification within the warranty period of defects in materials or workmanship, and such notification is determined by McGraw-Hill to be correct, McGraw-Hill will replace the defective CD ROM(s). Send request to:

Customer Service
McGraw-Hill
Gahanna Industrial Park
860 Taylor Station Road
Blacklick, OH 43004-9615

The entire and exclusive liability and remedy for breach of this Limited Warranty shall be limited to replacement of defective CD ROM(s) and shall not include or extend to any claim for or right to cover any other damages, including but not limited to, loss of profit, data, or use of the software, or special, incidental, or consequential damages or other similar claims, even if McGraw-Hill has been specifically advised as to the possibility of such damages. In no event will McGraw-Hill's liability for any damages to you or any other person exceed the lower of suggested list price or actual price paid for the license to use the Product, regardless of any form of the claim.

THE McGRAW-HILL COMPANIES, INC. SPECIFICALLY DISCLAIMS ALL OTHER WARRANTIES, EXPRESS OR IMPLIED, INCLUDING BUT NOT LIMITED TO, ANY IMPLIED WARRANTY OF MERCHANTABILITY OR FITNESS FOR A PARTICULAR PURPOSE. Specifically, McGraw-Hill makes no representation or warranty that the Product is fit for any particular purpose and any implied warranty of merchantability is limited to the sixty day duration of the Limited Warranty covering the physical CD ROM(s) only (and not the software or information) and is otherwise expressly and specifically disclaimed.

This Limited Warranty gives you specific legal rights; you may have others which may vary from state to state. Some states do not allow the exclusion of incidental or consequential damages, or the limitation on how long an implied warranty lasts, so some of the above may not apply to you.

This Agreement constitutes the entire agreement between the parties related to use of the Product. The terms of any purchase order shall have no effect on the terms of this Agreement. Failure of McGraw-Hill to insist at any time on strict compliance with this Agreement shall not constitute a waiver of any rights under this Agreement. This Agreement shall be construed and governed in accordance with the laws of New York. If any provision of this Agreement is held to be contrary to law, that provision will be enforced to the maximum extent permissible and the remaining provisions will remain in force and effect.